FROM LITERATURE TO BITERATURE

FROM

LITERATURE

TO

BITERATURE

Lem, Turing, Darwin, and Explorations in Computer Literature,
Philosophy of Mind, and Cultural Evolution

PETER SWIRSKI

McGill-Queen's University Press
Montreal & Kingston • London • Ithaca

© McGill-Queen's University Press 2013

ISBN 978-0-7735-4295-2 (cloth)
ISBN 978-0-7735-8991-9 (ePDF)
ISBN 978-0-7735-8992-6 (ePUB)

Legal deposit third quarter 2013
Bibliothèque nationale du Québec

Printed in Canada on acid-free paper that is 100% ancient forest free (100% post-consumer recycled), processed chlorine free

This book has been published with the help of a grant from the Canadian Federation for the Humanities and Social Sciences, through the Awards to Scholarly Publications Program, using funds provided by the Social Sciences and Humanities Research Council of Canada.

McGill-Queen's University Press acknowledges the support of the Canada Council for the Arts for our publishing program. We also acknowledge the financial support of the Government of Canada through the Canada Book Fund for our publishing activities.

Library and Archives Canada Cataloguing in Publication

Swirski, Peter, 1963–, author
    From literature to biterature : Lem, Turing, Darwin, and explorations in computer literature, philosophy of mind, and cultural evolution / Peter Swirski.

Includes bibliographical references and index.
Issued in print and electronic formats.
ISBN 978-0-7735-4295-2 (bound). – ISBN 978-0-7735-8991-9 (ePDF). – ISBN 978-0-7735-8992-6 (ePUB)

    1. Computers and civilization. 2. Artificial intelligence. 3. Social evolution. 4. Literature – Philosophy. 5. Philosophy of mind. 6. Language and languages – Philosophy. I. Title.

QA76.9.c66s94 2013   303.48'34   C2013-902978-8
                                           C2013-902979-6

This book was typeset by True to Type in 10.5/13 Baskerville

Dedicated to Jaakko Hintikka, Sami Pihlström,
David Livingstone Smith, and other bibliosophers
of today and tomorrow

Contents

FROM LITERATURE TO BITERATURE

Since most of the statements in this book are speculations, it would have been too tedious to mention this on every page. Instead I did the opposite – by taking out all words like "possibly" and deleting every reference to scientific evidence. Accordingly, this book should be read less as a text of scientific scholarship and more as an adventure story for the imagination. Each idea should be seen not as a firm hypothesis about the mind, but as another implement to keep inside one's toolbox for making theories of the mind.

Marvin Minsky

Lemmata

Narrative Intelligence; Test of Time; Avocados or Wombats;
Institute for Advanced Studies; Builtware and Bitware;
Paignton Zoo

NARRATIVE INTELLIGENCE

The first general-purpose – Turing-complete, in geekspeak – electronic brain was a behemoth of thirty-plus tons, roughly the same as an eighteen-wheeler truck. With twenty thousand vacuum tubes in its belly, it occupied a room the size of a college gym and consumed two hundred kilowatts, or about half the power of a roadworthy semi. Turn on the ignition, gun up the digital rig, and off you go, roaring and belching smoke on the information highway.

Running, oddly, on the decimal rather than the binary number system, the world's first Electronic Integrator and Computer also boasted a radical new feature: it was reprogrammable. It could, in other words, execute a variety of tasks by means of what we would call different software (in reality, its instructions were stored on kludgy manual plug-and-socket boards). Soldered together in 1946 by John Mauchly and J. Presper Eckert at the University of Pennsylvania, the ENIAC was a dream come true.

It was also obsolete before it was completed. The computer revolution had begun.

The rest is history as we know it. In less than a single lifetime, ever more powerful computing machines have muscled in on almost all facets of our lives, opening new vistas for operations and research on a daily basis. As I type this sentence, there are more than seven billion people in the world and more than two billion

Soldered together in 1946 by John Mauchly and J. Presper Eckert at the
University of Pennsylvania, the ENIAC was a dream come true.

computers – including the one on which I have just typed this sentence. And, by dint of typing it, I have done my bit to make the
word "computer" come up in written English more frequently than
99 per cent of all the nouns in the language.

   In a blink of an eye, computers have become an industry, not
merely in terms of their manufacture and design but in terms of
analysis of their present and future potential. The key factor behind
this insatiable interest in these icons of our civilization is their
cross-disciplinary utility. The computer and the cognitive sciences
bestraddle an ever-expanding miscellany of disciplines with fingers
in everything from alphanumerical regex to zettascale linguistics.

   Chief among them are artificial intelligence, artificial emotion,
artificial life, machine learning, knowledge engineering, software
engineering, robotics, electronics, vision, computability, information science – all with their myriad subfields. Towards the periphery,
they snake in and out of genetic algorithms, Boolean logic, neurol-
ogy and neuropathology, natural language processing, cognitive
and evolutionary psychology, decision and game theory, linguistics,
philosophy of mind, translation theory, and *their* myriad subfields.

So swift has been the expansion of computers' algorithmic and robotic capacities that quite a few of the assumptions forged in their formative decades no longer suffice to grasp their present-day potential, to say nothing about the future. This has never been truer than in our millennium in which research subdisciplines such as Narrative Intelligence are finally, if slowly, beginning to crawl out from the shadow of more established domains of Artificial Intelligence.

Underwriting this new field is mounting evidence from the biological and social sciences that a whole lot of cognitive processing is embedded in our natural skill for storytelling. As documented by psychologists, sociobiologists, and even literary scholars who have placed *Homo narrativus* under the microscope, we absorb, organize, and process information better when it is cast in the form of a story. We remember and retrieve causally framed narratives much better than atomic bits of RAM.

The power of the narrative is even more apparent in our striking bias toward contextual framing at the expense of the underlying logic of a situation. People given fifty dollars experience a sense of gain or loss – and change their behaviour accordingly – depending on whether they get to keep twenty or must surrender thirty. Equally, we fall prey to cognitive illusions when processing frequencies as probabilities rather than natural frequencies. A killer disease that wipes out 1,280 people out of 10,000 looms worse than one that kills 24.14 per cent, even though bug number 2 is actually twice as lethal.

Given such deep-seated cognitive lapses, the idea of grafting an artsy-fartsy domain such as storytelling onto digital computing may at first appear to be iffy, if not completely stillborn. Appearances, however, can be deceiving. The marriage of the computer sciences and the humanities is only the next logical step in the paradigm shift that is inclining contemporary thinkers who think about thinking to think more and more in terms of narratives rather than logic-gates. The narrative perspective on the ghost in the machine, it turns out, is not a speculative luxury but a pressing necessity.

TEST OF TIME

This is where *From Literature to Biterature* comes in. Underlying my explorations is the premise that, at a certain point in the already foreseeable future, computers will be able to create works of literature in and of themselves. What conditions would have to obtain for machines to become capable of creative writing? What would be the literary, cultural, and social consequences of these singular capacities? What role would evolution play in this and related scenarios? These are some of the central questions that preoccupy me in the chapters to come.

Fortunately, even if the job is enormous, I am not starting from zero. In *Of Literature and Knowledge* (2007) I devoted an entire book to the subject of narrative intelligence – *human* narrative intelligence. Evolution has bequeathed our species with a cunning array of cognitive skills to navigate the currents of life. Human intelligence is uniquely adapted to thought-experiment about the future and to data-mine the past – in short, to interpret and reinterpret context-sensitive information.

But what about machine intelligence? Is it a *sui generis* different kind of animal or just an offshoot of the main branch? And how does one calibrate intelligence in computers or even determine that it is there at all? Most of all, isn't machine intelligence, like military intelligence, an archetypal oxymoron? Jokes aside, it is not, because human and machine evolutions are ultimately two phases of the same process.

Bioevolution may have spawned technoevolution, but the accelerating pace of scientific discovery makes it all but certain that humanity is destined to take evolution into its own hands. From that point on, the difference between what is natural and artificial will begin to dissolve. Bioevolution will become a subfield of technoevolution inasmuch as the latter will facilitate steered – i.e., teleological – *autoevolution*. The evolutionary equilibrium of our species will have been punctuated in a most dramatic way. Biology will have become a function of biotech.

On the literary front, computers capable of writing fiction bring us face to face with the gnarly problems of authorship and intentionality. Both lie at the heart of my *Literature, Analytically Speaking* (2010), which brings order to the riot of positions and presuppositions around the matter of human art. This time around, my targets are authorial *in*tention and *ex*tension as they pertain to machines, albeit machines of a very different order from the mindless text-compilers of today: creative, artful, and causally independent.

I made a first pass at unlocking the riddles of computer authorship (or computhorship) and bitic literature (or biterature) in *Between Literature and Science* (2000). Much of what I wrote there has weathered the test of time better than I could have imagined. To take only one example, my analysis of the pragmatic factors in the administration of the Turing test, such as the role of perfect and complete information available to the judges, was independently developed in the same year by the cognitive scientist Ayse Saygin.

The success of these earlier studies gives me the confidence to trespass onto the territory staked out by computer scientists and roboticists, even if it is in pursuit of inquiries that might be, on balance, of more interest to literary scholars and philosophers. Seen in this light, *From Literature to Biterature* is not a book of science, even though some humanists may find it overly technical for their taste. Nor is it a book of literary theory, even as it liberally trucks in narrative cases and critical lore. It is rather an old-fashioned book of discovery or, if you prefer, a modern adventure story of the mind.

AVOCADOS OR WOMBATS

While books on digital literature are no longer as hard to find as they were in the days of Espen Aarseth's *Cybertext* (1997), literary-critical voyages to the digital shores of tomorrow are as still rare as a steak that runs on four legs. This includes the self-styled exception to the rule, a cheerleading overview of computer-assisted writing, Katherine Hayles's *Electronic Literature* (2008). Limited by and large to a survey of second-order mashing protocols of yesterday, it stands in sharp contrast to my anatomy of electronic literature of tomorrow.

The aim of my explorations, the first of their kind, is simple. I want to draw a synoptic map of the future in which the gulf concealed by the term "bitic literature" – that is, the gulf between mere syntax-driven processing and semantically rich understanding – has been bridged. As it happens, the gulf in question is greater than that which separates tree-climbing pygmy marmosets from the Mbenga and Mbuti human pygmy tribes of Central Africa. As such, the ramifications of this single lemma could hardly be more far-reaching.

Most conspicuously, acknowledging biterature as a species of literature entails adopting the same range of attitudes to computhors as to human writers. Specifically, it entails approaching them as agents with internal states, such as, for instance, creative intentions. Here, however, we find ourselves on shaky ground. Computers with creative intentions are perforce computers that think, but what is the status of such thinking? Are machine thoughts and intentions real, like avocados or wombats, or are they merely useful theoretical fictions, like centres of gravity or actuarial averages?

These questions breed other questions like neutrons in a runaway chain reaction. Is thinking in computers different from that in humans? What would it mean if it turned out to be radically different or, for that matter, not different at all? Can machines *really* think, or is thinking merely what we could *attribute* to advanced future systems? And what does *really* really mean in this context, given that thinking about thinking machines segues seamlessly into thinking about machines with personality, identity, karma, and God knows what else?

INSTITUTE FOR ADVANCED STUDIES

As I work my way through this thicket of questions, I hitch a ride on the shoulders of three thinkers who have, in their respective ways, mapped out the contours of this *terra incognita*. First on the list is Stanislaw Lem. One of the greatest novelists of the twentieth century, he was also one of the most far-sighted philosophers of tomorrow, lionized by Mr Futurology himself, Alvin Toffler (of *Future Shock* fame). Not coincidentally, Lem is also the author of the only existing map of the literary future, patchy and dated though it may seem today.

But even as *From Literature to Biterature* is a book about literature, it is not a book of literary exegesis. The difference is fundamental. Throughout Lem's career, reviewers marvelled at the complexity and scientific erudition of his scenarios, eulogizing him as a literary Einstein and a science-fiction Bach. His novels and thought experiments, exclaimed one critic, read "as if they were developed at Princeton's Institute for Advanced Studies."[1]

Maybe, maybe not. For how would you know? Literary critics hardly flock to Princeton to get a degree in the computer or evolutionary sciences in order to find out if Lem's futuristic scenarios are right or, indeed, wrong. Not a few contend, in fact, that this is

Most conspicuously, acknowledging biterature as a specics of literature entails adopting the same range of attitudes to computhors as to human writers. Specifically, it entails approaching them as agents with internal states, such as, for instance, creative intentions.

the way it ought to be, inasmuch as literary studies are not even congruent with the cognitive orientation of the sciences – cognitive, biological, or any other. If so, I purposely step outside the confines of literary criticism by affording Lem the conceptual scrutiny he deserves, in the process tweaking his hypotheses or rewriting them altogether.

If Alan Turing's name is synonymous with machine intelligence, it is as much for his contributions to cognitive science as for his unshakable belief in intelligent machines – *contra* John von Neumann, who was as unshakably certain they would never think. From Turing machines to the Turing Award (the most prestigious prize for computer scientists), down to the Turing Police, who lock horns with a supercomputer that plots to boost its intelligence in William Gibson's modern sci-fi classic *Neuromancer* – his name pops up everywhere.

Celebrated as one of *Time's* "100 Persons of the [Twentieth] Century," to this day Turing is regarded as a prophet of machine intelligence. More than sixty years after it was unveiled, his test remains the single most consequential contribution to our thinking about thinking computers. Appropriately, the 2012 celebrations of the Turing Year even comprised a special Turing test conducted at Bletchley Park outside London, where the British mathematician played such a decisive role in decoding German military ciphers during World War II.

In many ways, the Turing test forms the backbone of the book in your hands. Although the protocol itself and all the Chinese Room-type critiques of it are by now nothing new, I squeeze a fair amount of juice out of the old orange by going at it from a novel angle, while adding a bunch of new twists to old themes. Indeed, as I argue throughout, the test itself is a categorically different tool – inductive rather than analytic – from what almost every analyst claims it to be.

As for Charles Darwin, I assume you don't need to be told who he was and why he matters. Let me just say that, even though *From Literature to Biterature* is not a book of fiction, it fashions a hero of epic proportions: evolution. No one can tell what role evolution will play in future computer design, but my bet is that it will be substantial. My other bet is that natural selection itself may be due for an overhaul as laws of self-organization and autocatalysis supplement what we know of this fundamental force that orders our living universe.

Chiefly, although not exclusively, the last part of the book thus spins a series of scenarios that leave the present-day world far behind. My basic premise is that computer evolution will by its very nature exceed the pace of natural evolution a thousand- or even a million-fold. Being, at the same time, directed by the machines themselves, it will leave its imprint on every page of the book of life as we know it. Whether these scenarios qualify as literary futurology, evolutionary speculation, or philosophy of the future I leave for you to judge.

BUILTWARE AND BITWARE

Before we hoist anchor, a few words on a few key terms and mental shortcuts necessary to navigate the book in your hands. Let me start with those that crop up on almost every page: *thinking, intelligence, understanding,* and to a lesser extent *consciousness.* Given that each is loaded with connotations – especially in philosophy and psychology, where they are sometimes glossed as *having semantics* or *having intentionality* – right off the bat I disclaim any meanings that go outside their common usage.

Taking all these descriptors to denote simply the cognitive abilities of a normal human being, I also take them to be synonymous and interchangeable: if you have one, you have the others. Just like rationality, intelligence has long been seen as strung evenly on a single axis, with geniuses at one end and blondes at the other. Not so – at least not since 1983, when psychologist Howard Gardner distinguished no less than seven types of intelligence: linguistic, logical-mathematical, bodily-kinaesthetic, social-interpersonal, introspective-intrapersonal, musical, and spatial.

Having said that, I take reasoned response to change to be a necessary, though not necessarily sufficient, condition for intelligence. Not coincidentally, this prima facie AI characterization can be easily reinterpreted in biological terms. This is because reasoning (memory, analysis, and prediction), fortified by feedback and performance evaluation, belongs to a suite of cognitive adaptations to sort out all manner of environmental stimuli in the service of homeostasis and self-preservation.

Finally, a few words on the star player: the computer. Speaking of computer performance is always a matter of metaphor and metonymy or, if you prefer, colloquial convenience. This is because the actual physical aggregate of circuits called hardware is not, in and of itself, capable of anything. The same is true of software. Long or short, strings of binary digits – or bits, as they have been called since Claude Shannon's 1948 breakthrough paper on the mathematical theory of communication – that form a computer's chain of instructions have, in and of themselves, no causal powers.

Sitting on a shelf, whether in the form of magnetic pulses or symbols on paper, a "disembodied" program is incapable of executing anything at all, be it a series of legal manoeuvres to probate an estate or a timed release of a lethal cocktail into the vein of a death-row inmate. To have any computing or causal powers, both the bitware and the builtware must act as one. Decoupled, neither is capable of affecting its internal or external environment.

PAIGNTON ZOO

Talking about implementation or even evolution of programs *in* computers presupposes a strict division of hardware and software. Replace the processors with other processors, for example, and the software should remain intact. Not so in biological evolution, where brain software and hardware evolved in unison. Prefrontal cortex, to take one example, is responsible for growth in abstract thinking – implicated in tool-making, culture, social practices, and so on – and is at the same time a co-evolutionary outgrowth of our capabilities for language, art, and awareness of mortality.

If in what follows I stick, therefore, to the term *computer*, it is only as a handy shorthand for the embodied software of a fully integrated program-processor-effector. Naturally, future science may yet erase the entire software-hardware divide, bringing computer manufacture and design conspicuously in line with human manufacture and design. In a homology to human reproductive cells, which in anthropogenesis combine the functions of morphological building blocks and ontogenetic blueprints, our bitware and builtware may one day also collapse into one.

Unfortunately, it is not uncommon for such futuristic speculation to drive our collective head only deeper into the sand. For the societal ostrich, visions of autonomous autotelic automata are hard to square with the kludgy clunkers of today which make even Paignton Zoo macaques look like a troop of Dostoyevskys. Presented in 2003 with a keyboard connected to a PC, after a month of labours the six monkeys managed to bang out five pages of the letter "S" and break the keyboard.

Nothing to worry about, in other words, since the future will look a lot like today, only a little more so. Take Poe's "Mellonta Tauta" at face value, and in the year 2048 we will race around in giant balloons at neck-breaking speeds of 150 miles an hour. The flip side of this sort of escapism, on the other hand, is not realism but fantasy in which the future extrapolates itself into Asimov's asinine three "laws" of robotics or a doomsday script out of Schwarzenegger's *Terminator 3: Rise of the Machines*.

In the place of bad science fiction, however, we need good science and good fiction aimed at the socio-cultural, aesthetic, ethical, and even ontological implications of the ghost in the machine. As one of Shakespeare's memorable creations said on encountering a ghost outside the machine, there are more things in heaven and earth than are dreamt of in our philosophy. Truly, we may need to rethink our philosophy, both natural and analytic, if the computer is to help us create a better and not just a faster society.

Not for a moment do I mean to suggest that the scenarios I conjure up in the pages that follow are in any way inevitable or even desirable. It is far from a foregone conclusion that my hypotheses will morph from fiction to fact. I do mean, however, to dispute the default perception that they can't happen here. After all, we have only begun to scratch the surface of tomorrow. But from where I'm standing, the scratches are getting deeper by the minute, looking more and more like gouges.

PART ONE

Lem's intuitive and literary approach perhaps does a better job of convincing readers to his views than any hard-nosed scientific article or arcanely reasoned philosophical paper might do.

Douglas R. Hofstadter and Daniel Dennnett

Biterature

Toscanelli's Map; Bloomsday; Titan; Manchester Mark;
Manglers and Mashers; Suits for the Dawn Patrol; Charabia;
Short for Raconteur; I Gave Myself an Electric Current; Abe's
Saloon!; Humming (to Itself?)

TOSCANELLI'S MAP

Before he ventured into the uncharted waters of the Atlantic, Columbus armed himself with the famous Toscanelli map, which sketched the route to the Spice Islands of Asia. A smart move, except that, even as the parchment represented the distillate of the best geographical intelligence of the time, it was in equal measure a fanciful projection of the cartographer's imagination. As a matter of fact, Toscanelli had badly miscalculated the size of the Earth, which is why Columbus never realized that he had stumbled on an unknown continent.

Even a fanciful map may be better than none, however, when voyaging to a place on the continuum where everything by default is a projection of the cartographer's imagination. Hence, as I venture into the uncharted waters populated by such chimeras as biterary computhors, I take advantage of a singular map of the future. First published in 1973, Lem's "A History of Bitic Literature" (released in English as part of *Imaginary Magnitude*) is a singular work of fiction by any standard. It takes the form of a metafictional preface to a proleptic review of computer writing from the year 2009. His future, our past.

Similarly to Turing's legendary essay "On Computable Numbers," Lem's opens with a definition. Biterature, he writes, is "any work of

nonhuman origin – one whose *real* author is not a human being."[1]
The very next sentence, however, executes a dramatic U-turn. Now
Lem allows that humans could author biterature *indirectly* "by performing the functions which generated the real author's acts of creation." For the record, he is not alone in hedging his bets in this
way. In his Pulitzer-winning meditations on the nature of computer
consciousness, *Gödel, Escher, Bach* (1979), Douglas Hofstadter also
distinguished the real author from meta-author.

Taken separately, the two concepts make good sense. On the one
hand there is the real author – the creator who brings a novel into
existence – and on the other there is the intellectual entourage:
people who for a variety of reasons have influenced his artistic
development and creative process. Fuse the two concepts together,
however, and they blow the concept of biterary authorship out of
the sky. This is so because Lem's indirect author doubles back on
the real author, calling *both* concepts into question. Suddenly the
issue of authorship can no longer be resolved without bringing the
intellectual entourage into the picture.

From Lem's theses it follows that any author, human or not, is
only the terminal stage in the genesis of a work. The crippling lack
of what programmers call a "stopping rule" is easier to grasp on
examples from the world of our flesh-and-blood creators. In Lem's
view, writers are only conventional bookends for their teachers,
mentors, colleagues, writers, critics, and anybody else who might
have indirectly contributed to the genesis of their work. That's
right: anybody who played *any* role in the nominal author's creation becomes an indirect author of the resulting work.

This makes no sense. Take the droll scenario from Martin Ritt's
1976 satirical comedy, *The Front*. In a rare acting-only appearance,
Woody Allen plays Howard Prince, an amiable schmo who during
the 1950s' HUAC witch-hunts fronts for a group of scriptwriters
branded as pinkos. In return, Howard gets the publishing credits
and a cut of the royalties, and everybody is happy (until the schmo
begins to demand revisions to fit "his" style).

Is Howard an indirect author of the scripts that bear his name?
If you think that the answer is a no-brainer – he never pens a word
– remember that without him no word would get penned in the
first place. In his way, Howard plays an indispensable role in the
genesis of the scripts, exactly as prescribed by Lem's protocol. That
role is not dissimilar to that of every commissioning editor who, by

Is Howard an indirect author of the scripts that bear his name? If you think that the answer is a no-brainer – he never pens a word – remember that without him no word would get penned in the first place.

dint of issuing a publishing contract, performs a key function in the process of creation.

Thus, if we were to take Lem's theses in good faith, the publishing house of Little, Brown who commissioned Norman Mailer to write a book-length account of Apollo 11's epochal mission would thus become an author, albeit an indirect one, of Mailer's work. Make room on the shelf for *Of a Fire on the Moon* by Mailer, Little, and Brown, all because their contract played a generative function in the history of the book. Without it, this fine piece of new journalism would presumably have never got written.

BLOOMSDAY

It should be evident by now why, by adding a rider to his first clause, Lem generates more headaches than he cures. What is missing from his account of computer authorship is causal depth: the *actual* and *direct* causal mechanism needed to save the entire concept from being true but trivial or true but insufficient. In short, we need some kind of rule that will separate Little, Brown from standing too closely behind, or Howard Prince from standing in front of, the actual writer.

No less problematically, Lem's definition locks itself into a potentially infinite regress. After all, the circle of influence around literary authors is every inch arbitrary. Just as all authors are influenced by people around them, all the people who contribute to these authors' output are influenced by other people, who themselves are influenced by others still, and so on, and so forth. Once you let indirect authorship into the picture, you end up with a labyrinth of reciprocal influences extending spatially and temporally in all directions.

With a stroke of a pen, Lem has created something like a demented Derridean paradise – a pan-textual allegory of literary meanings and influences dispersed in an infinite playground of intercausality. The patent absurdity of the whole idea is best brought out by examples from our world. James Joyce's *Ulysses* (book edition 1922) is indisputably influenced by Homer's *Odyssey*. Does this make Homer an indirect author of Leopold and Molly Bloom?

Not nutty enough? How about Homer being an indirect author of "Gigamesh," a story published in Lem's 1971 collection *A Perfect Vacuum*? The whole point of this fictive review of a fictive novel by a fictive Irishman, Patrick Hannahan, is that it is shot through with references and allusions to *Ulysses* and *Finnegans Wake*. Feted by Joyce's fans on the annual Bloomsday (June 16), *Ulysses* clearly played an influential role in Lem's "Gigamesh," while – let us not forget – having been indirectly authored by the Blind One. The inference is as clear-cut as a cattle ranch that used to be rainforest: transitively, Homer is an indirect author of "Gigamesh."

The whole thing is, of course, utter nonsense. There was no James Joyce, no Dublin, no Ireland, no United States, no Library of Congress, no World War II, no GI Joes, no digital computers, and no Boltzmann's constant in Homer's antiquity. Yet all of them figure in Lem's story, of which the Greek bard was, by virtue of this deranged anachronistic calculus, an indirect author.

TITAN

Fabricating a world wide web of influences extending in all four dimensions, indirect authorship contravenes the very foundations of our social and cultural practices. The judicial or economic consequences alone – for example, those concerning property and copyright laws, or royalties and work-for-hire statutes – would call its hallucinatory axioms into question. From any point of view, analytic or commonsensical, the notion of indirect authorship is just plain silly.

Swing the pendulum a half-period, however, and you end up with no less nonsense. To embrace the antithetical view, namely that the terminal stage of literary production is the only one that counts, is to neglect the human factor in all forms of today's electronic writing. Since the text file of the book you are now reading was generated using iMac hardware and Word software, would you be prepared to argue that the iMac-Word team wrote *From Literature to Biterature*? I hope not!

To sort out the mess of causal connections between computer creators and creations, we need to distinguish three orders of authorship. Based on the degree of independence from human control, the schema is at once synchronic and diachronic. Not surprisingly, being most indebted to human programmers, text-slotters of the first order were the first to appear on the scene. At the end of the day, of course, they are no more writers than a pair of dice is.

At this level, textual output takes place entirely within so-called closed forms, the writing and running of which involve maximum oversight from the programmer. The computer's role is limited to slotting more or less rigorously determined textual variables into preselected gaps in a prescribed frame. Think of the whole protocol as dressing up a Christmas tree – more or less at random. The human Santa supplies the tree and the assortment of verbal baubles, while the source code spins the big wheel to determine whether the red bow will go on branch 6 and the miniature snowman on branch 2, or vice versa.

In principle, any randomizing device such as a Caesar's Palace roulette wheel could be used to perform this combinatorial function. Not surprisingly, the whole idea is a bit old hat – a Chinese coolie hat, to be exact. *I Ching*, the world's oldest book of divination, is more than three thousand years old and a perfect example of randomly generated text. Employing the traditional yarrow stalks or the modern three-coin toss (which actually changes the probabilities), the system can be cast for hexagrams said to reward inquirers with a reflection of the universe in miniature.

In eighteenth-century central Europe, another popular dice-based system called *Musikalisches Würspiel* was employed to string together short compositions from a stock of musical phrases, which were then performed by hired players. Today, the standard iPod shuffle lets listeners create a kaleidoscope of new playlists from old songs while the cross-fade can in principle generate any number of novel musical phrases.

At the risk of restating the obvious, the tripartite ordering of computer authorship has nothing to do with processing capacity and everything with the use to which a system is put. Take Tianhe-1A, the world's fourth-fastest processor, housed at the National Supercomputing Center in Tianjin, or Japan's third-fastest Fujitsu K model, or the American runner-up Sequoia, or Cray's Titan, the current champ. Clocked in at speeds measured in petaflops – that's numbers followed by fourteen zeros of floating point operations per second – they could claim the title of the world's fleetest text-slotters if equipped with the right sort of software.

MANCHESTER MARK

First-order text-compilers go back to the computer's infancy. Historically, the laurels belong to the Manchester Mark 1 – a prototype for Ferranti's Mark 1 which beat UNIVAC by a month for the title of the world's first commercial general-purpose electronic computer. (Neither of these two Marks should be confused with IBM's electro-mechanical Mark 1 put together by Howard Aitken's team in 1944 to generate ordnance tables for American units still fighting in Europe and in the Pacific.)

In a little-known literary experiment from 1952, the Manchester Mark 1 became the first documented computer "writer" by generating a love letter with a little more than a little help from its programmers. The team of Alan Turing and Chris Strachey used the random number generator – one of Turing's few contributions to the design of the Manchester machine – to assemble, among others, this *billet doux*:

First-order text-compilers go back to the computer's infancy. Historically, the laurels belong to the Manchester Mark 1 – a prototype for Ferranti's Mark 1 that beat UNIVAC by a month for the title of the world's first commercial general-purpose electronic computer.

Darling Sweetheart,
You are my avid feeling. My affection curiously clings to your passionate wish. My liking yearns to your heart. You are my wistful sympathy: my tender liking.

Owing to Turing's enthusiastic – not to say propagandistic – copy, the British press reported widely on the operations of the machine, referring to it, according to the custom of the time, as an "electronic brain." All this touched a raw nerve with a prominent neurosurgeon, Geoffrey Jefferson, in what would be the opening salvo of a decades-long war of words as to whether a computer could ever be creative. Turing took note. In his game-changing 1950 article, "Computing Machinery and Intelligence," he quoted from the central part of Jefferson's peroration as an example of Objection from Consciousness.

Incapable of contributing anything in and of themselves, text-compilers are, ultimately, puppets in the hands of the programmer who determines their performance. Broadly speaking, they fall into two classes. At one end of the spectrum, the source-code simply slots word tokens into a man-made frame. Depending on the script, it may prompt you en route for a list of nouns, verbs, adverbs, or adjectives before spitting out the word salad tossed to your liking. Somewhat more ambitiously, it may generate copy from scratch using dictionaries and subroutines that in a rudimentary fashion control the flow of syntax.

The competing approach is – in technical jargon – to mangle or mash existing text to get a new one. After all, making computers understand human code is difficult, but making them manipulate is not. In the olden days, when human artists did their mashing by hand, the technique went by the name of aleatory or Dadaist writing. White noise, random generators, mechanical composition, free association, automatism: anything to outrage the bourgeois public accustomed to coherent *objets d'art*. Today it is called computer-generated writing, or CGW.

MANGLERS AND MASHERS

Mangling or, if you prefer, creative rewriting techniques can vary to a great extent, depending on your skill, patience, or ingenuity. Take a text, any text, drop it down a rabbit hole of one of the manglers freely available online, and watch it come up autistic on the other side. The ways to Dadaicize writing are myriad. Some scripts even offer advanced filters that successfully simulate neuropathologies ranging from dyslexia to stuttering.

Here are two low-tech protocols you can try at home. Scan a text on low resolution, then run a spellcheck, and iterate back and forth until you get the verbal eggs scrambled to your satisfaction. The other approach is even simpler and more fun. Feed the source text into the Google translator and grind it over allopatric languages until you get a verbal soufflé that looks like it was hatched by the Swedish chef from *The Muppet Show*. Here is the paragraph you have just read, mangled five times over in the manner I have just described:

There are two short cans to the home health minute try. Clear
text short resolution, and then run the spelling check and Woo

have been back and forth several times until you get an egg
your makuusi. Oral easier in seconds and more fun. The source
code to convert the service to Google and grinding allopatrik
more languages, until you get a pop-verbal puppet seems, even
the Swedish Chief. Here are some of you just read, but more
than five times the method described sliced.

Some protocols for generating without originating are more
original than others, and here is one that might even have literary
potential: hybridize two or more texts that would not normally go
together. Start, for example, with the narrative frame and syntax of
The Canterbury Tales but replace the verbs and adjectives with those
culled from the gangsta rap of 2Pac Shakur. Yo, Wife of Bath,
Wonda why they call U bitch?

No need to stop there. Like a mad genreticist, you could elec-
tronically graft hard-boiled diction onto doctor-nurse melodrama,
spice up Henry James's *Daisy Miller* with a dash of Hemingway's *The
Sun Also Rises*, spike neo-classicism with the baroque, romanticize
the medievals, ultra-modernize Shakespeare – all to various aleatory, comic, or even aesthetically noteworthy purposes. A particularly thoughtful programmer could even turn such xenography into
a novelty publishing goldmine, if perhaps not exactly a Nobel
Prize.

SUITS FOR THE DAWN PATROL

For intrinsic reasons, things are even more mangle-friendly in lyri-
cal poetry where the information-bearing function of a language is
suppressed, or even entirely sacrificed, in the name of symbolically subjective expression. The results run osculatory to standard
discourse – without, it must be said, necessarily becoming meaningless.

Naturally, past a certain point semantic eccentricity will make it
well nigh impossible to differentiate random assembly from the
allusive end of the human spectrum. Take a look at the following
free verse. Is it human or computer mash?

enormous parking lot four floors under cement bare plaster
asthmatic bulbs black the men sallow to match garments
before eyes bored on him listless assignments familiar the
speech words with precision of machine gun no more machine

guns no bullets no production any more on the stairs suited
hobnailed soles two halfdragging third torn suits weaponless
dumped him unceremonious in the remote corner on a heap
dumped unceremonious in the remote corner muscular
freeing hand bitten off all fingers gushing blood told him
to move his fucking ass stare stump hand cold coarse cement
nobody heeded survivor intention to recount several phrases
without enthusiasm fighting suits for the dawn patrol

Whatever your answer is, would you be terribly surprised if it
turned out to be the other? The same question hangs, of course,
over much, perhaps even most, of the postmodernist critical
canon. Consider the following two paragraphs of theorese. One is
transcribed verbatim from Jean Baudrillard's classic 1981 essay,
"Simulacra and Simulation," while the other has been mindlessly
assembled by a mangler script. See whether you can tell which is
which.[2]

And just as much in an inverse, irreversible, implosive process:
a generalised deterrence of the social order is engendered, well
beyond all relations of force, a stake – this is nothing more
than the critical obsession with its aura of transgression, of
order, with its aura of an offence, is the horizon between reality,
and to die under the sign as value from the political sphere is
signaled.

In this passage to a space whose curvature is no longer that
of the real, nor of truth, the age of simulation thus begins
with liquidation of all referentials – worse: by their artificial
resurrection in systems of signs, which are a more ductile material than meaning, in that they lend themselves to all systems
of equivalence, all binary oppositions and all combinatory
algebra.

CHARABIA

Online scripts that generate philosophical fodder of this sort have
been around for decades. Not surprisingly, they tend to capitalize
on the continental rather than the analytic tradition, although
some can apparently whip up serviceable "appreciations" of Witt-

genstein, as testified to by "yr p.gram svd my lf" blogs from philosophy undergrads. Other online text-spinners churn out rants,
abuse-a-trons, surreal compliments, experimental cooking recipes,
sensational tabloid headlines, and – not least – haikus by the met-
ric tonne.

The open-endedness of the Japanese form, only loosely constrained by imagistic juxtapositions within the 5–7–5 syllabic pattern, is tailor-made for machine mash. *Charabia*, a French-language
site dedicated to the *génération automatique de textes aléatoires*, is one
of many that dish them out at a click of a mouse. Patiently, the
script slots variables from a ready-made set of words and phrases
into the syllabic frame, to the delight of poetasters worldwide.

In August 2011, the slot machine rewarded me with the following two quasi-haikus in a row (they did not scan in the original
either):

Evening rain
Rustles the snow
Tired, I put down my baguettes.

Sleeping sun
Waves afloat
Tired, I put down my baguettes.

Note that "baguettes" is critically ambiguous, insofar as it can
also mean "chopsticks." In fact, the entire last line could be rendered as "Fatigued, I rest my chopsticks," opening a hermeneutical
bonanza for tenure-hungry exegetes of electronic literature. Their
mindset is perhaps best encapsulated by Louis Milic, one of the
early practitioners and theorists of machine mashing, who scoffed
at all those who scoffed at poetry compilers: "People who scoff at
computer poetry are simply not thinking."[3]

In a way, text generators do deserve a measure of praise, although not from aestheticians but from environmentalists. Mashing and mangling scripts exemplifies the green ethic. Nothing ever
gets thrown away, nothing ever gets wasted. Machine aleatorists will
use and reuse every word supplied to them, sort of like a mid-1997
Amazon store's promo that pledged John Updike to generate a
mystery story using paragraphs written by visitors to the site.

From the promotional angle, the contest was a smash hit. The volume of response overwhelmed Amazon's editorial staff, who had to plow through ten thousand fresh entries every day for a month and a half to pick the daily $1,000 winner to be added to the plot line. From the literary angle, on the other hand – replete though it is with references to Homer, Euripides, Poe, and Lewis Carroll – "Murder Makes the Magazine" by John Updike and The Surfers is erratic enough to have come from the *Choose Your Own Adventure* children's series.

SHORT FOR RACONTEUR

In contrast to the more-or-less rigidly controlled output of closed-form scripts, text-generators of the second order employ open formats. Starting with a set of sometimes only broadly delimited textual variables, the program strings words together without a necessarily prescribed sequence or even length. Needless to say, the borderline between the two types is not immutable or even clear-cut but is contextually dependent on the magnitude and nature of human intervention.

Still, as Bill Chamberlain – co-programmer (with Thomas Etter) of the most popular word synthesizer of this type – would have it, the differences are real. Human input, as he points out, is removed to some extent from the system's output. Even more to the point, such output "is no longer of a preprogrammed form; the computer forms it on its own, contingent upon what it finds in its files."[4] Of course, it is still the programmer who orchestrates the files and the protocol and, as such, the cleverness and/or quirkiness of the composition.

Never mind, counters Chamberlain. What comes out at the other end is quite "coherent and apparently thoughtful – crazily thoughtful, I grant you, but expressed in perfect English."[5] Granted, flawless syntax is far from a mean feat, given that the software generates and recombines not only individual words but phrases, paragraphs, and even larger generic or thematic elements. Even more to the point, perfect Oxford grammar nudges readers to search for coherence among semantic juxtapositions that, depending on the eye of the beholder, can range from the merely iconoclastic to the downright incongruous.

Since 1983, when Chamberlain and Etter published the first selection of verse and prose generated by their word synthesizer, their book has achieved the status of a minor cult classic. Hyped as the first book ever written by a computer, the skinny, squarish, coffee-table *The Policeman's Beard Is Half Constructed* was attributed to Racter (short for Raconteur), a Z80 micro with a pitiful-sounding 64 kilobytes of random-access memory. Nice gimmick, except that the genuine hilarity of the vignettes is a carefully orchestrated effect by man and not machine.

Since the commercial version of the program for MS-DOS platform is downloadable from the Endangered Software Archive, you can try interacting (pun intended!) with it at home. Quickly you will realize why, in the decades since, the script has not spawned anything remotely approaching the inspired lunacy of the original electronic rambler. Never mind whose name is on the cover: what counts is what is between the covers, and that depends entirely on the templates compiled by the programmers, plus on painstaking editing of the verbal diarrhoea cranked out by Racter.

I GAVE MYSELF AN ELECTRIC CURRENT

The general problem with interpreting second-order synthesizer output is that, preset by evolution for cooperative communication, our minds automatically seek to impose coherence on the text, no matter how scattered the syntax or semantics. Indeed, given a sufficiently dogged and imaginative exegete, there is no such thing as a meaningless text. Umberto Eco highlighted this point in his parody of deconstructive free-for-alls, *Foucault's Pendulum*, in which even non-existent messages carry truths for minds fixated on finding them.

Think back to Lewis Carroll's poem "Jabberwocky." In another place and another time, all those slithy toves that gyred and gimbled in the wabe could have been generated by a source code known as JABBERWACKY. Suppose for a minute that such is indeed the case, and that all the nonsense jabbering about mimsy borogroves and mome raths has been mindlessly stitched by an aluminium-encased word synthesizer and not by the socially inept British logician.

Now that you know that they were not meant to mean anything at all, are these odd, if perhaps oddly pleasing, lines merely oblique or plain obtuse? Are they deliciously playful or mangled and mal-

The First Book Ever Written by a Computer

THE POLICEMAN'S
BEARD
IS
HALF
CONSTRUCTED

Computer prose and poetry
by
Racter

Illustrations by Joan Hall

Introduction by William Chamberlain

A Bizarre and Fantastic Journey into the Mind of a Machine

Hyped as the first book ever written by a computer, the skinny, squarish, coffee-table *The Policeman's Beard Is Half Constructed* was attributed to Racter (short for Raconteur), a Z80 micro with a pitiful-sounding 64 kilobytes of random-access memory.

formed? Are you interacting with a literary gem or with patent gibberish? As you can see from this little thought experiment, the text alone does not determine the properties of an artwork. The material structures of a run-of-a-mill urinal and Duchamp's exhibit are identical, but their provenance and thus some of their aesthetic features are not.

Just as provenance and art-historical context affect perceptions and aesthetic qualities of human art, so they do for machine-spun literature. The following two *recits* from Racter adumbrate the point. Even though they are far from coherent, they are also far from incoherent. Their hilarity stems, in fact, from our automatic attempts to integrate the scattershot scripture by trying to make sense of the imagined intentions behind them.

> I gave the man a coat. I gave the woman a brassiere. I gave myself an electric current. We all were happy and full of delight. Take the coat from the man and remove the brassiere from the woman and take the electric current from me and we will be sad and full of anguish.

> Love is the question and the subject of this essay. We will commence with a question: does steak love lettuce? This question is implacably hard and inevitably difficult to answer. Here is a question: does an electron love a proton, or does it love a neutron? Here is a question: does a man love a woman or, to be specific, does Bill love Diane? The interesting and critical response to this question is: no! He is obsessed and infatuated with her. He is loony and crazy about her. That is not love of steak and lettuce, of electron and proton and neutron. This dissertation will show that the love of a man and a woman is not the love of steak and lettuce. Love is interesting to me and fascinating to you, but it is painful to Bill and Diane. That is love!

ABE'S SALOON!

Leaving computers aside for a moment, let us take a quick tour of second-order writing on the human side of the spectrum. Protocols for generating text at this level of creativity have been around since the dawn of literary criticism. Most, if not all, critical and metacritical essays are, in fact, efforts to formulate and formalize second-order compositional principles. Poe's mocking "How to Write a Blackwood Article" (1838) and his more straight-laced "The Philosophy of Composition" (1846) are quintessential examples of the genre.

Both are examples of what we would call heuristic rule sets that aim to articulate algorithms for a certain variety of open-form prose. "Blackwood," for instance, does so by mockingly dispensing tonal, modal, generic, thematic, and stylistic prescriptions that, in Poe's satire, characterize Blackwood prose. Primitive as these protocols may appear to us, in AI terms they are off the charts in terms of creation by imitation. As such, they are completely beyond the capacity of present-day systems to make use, or even make sense, of them.

Ever ready for literary mischief, Poe actually puts his prescriptions to work by composing a perfectly dreadful exemplar of a Blackwood story. Thus "A Predicament," published in 1838 jointly with "How to Write a Blackwood Article," cashes out in narrative form the tongue-in-cheek advice from the critical essay. Ostensibly composed by a Signora Psyche Zenobia, the story exemplifies the second-order heuristics "programmed" into the lady by the publisher, Mr Blackwood.

"A Predicament" is thus fashioned in a style heterogeneous, which, as Poe informs us, is at once laconic, elevated, and metaphysical – not to mention replete with sensations and sensationalism, piquant expressions, and flummery, as well as "a good spicing of the decidedly unintelligible." In the midst of this send-up of uncreative writing, Mr Blackwood even gives a thumbs-up to the idea of slotting variables into a ready-made frame. Any verbal scrap will do, he assures his audience, although "you must depend upon your own ingenuity to make it fit into your article."[6]

Good advice is never bad, and Mr Blackwood's heuristics are not that dissimilar to those that make the annual International Imitation Hemingway Competition – better known as the Bad Hemingway Contest – such a riot. The rules are simple. Entrants submit a one-page exemplar of Papa's style, and the most least accomplished of them wins the prize. Joseph Wambaugh and Ray Bradbury are only two of the thousands of parodists who over the years have taken a crack at running amok with Hemingway, to the appreciative groans of the judges and kibitzers.

Insofar as parody involves exaggerating salient characteristics out of proportion, it can be programmed into an algorithm designed to approximate the style of a given artist. Specimens of what I will generically dub EZ-Writer software are already up and running. In phase one the program is fed a sampling of works in order to formulate their language model. In phase two it employs this model to generate prose or verse in the style of the original. No more chasing the muse for inspiration, lineation, or alliteration for your trochaic triplets. At a click of the mouse the computer will compose your "Rhyme of the NASA Mariner" while you sit back, invisible, refined out of existence, indifferent, paring your fingernails.

It is easy to see how advanced EZ-Writers could eventually undermine all of our art-historical traditions and institutions. Just as some judges have already judged chatbots to be human beings in Turing-like tests, computer-written literature could well be judged to have been written by the imitated master. In a *Twilight Zone* scenario, it could even strike the writer as "his." It could lead to situations as bizarre as that in which Rembrandt found himself later in life when some of his paintings were being passed over for those of his disciple Govaert Flinck, the paying patrons deeming them to be more Rembrandt-like.

Having ingested and digested the selection of masterpieces and having analyzed their state space, the software can even produce reams of previously unknown drafts of, say, *The Old Man and the Sea* or *Absalom! Absalom!* I am only surprised that someone has not tried it yet. Then again, judging by some of the winners of the Bad Hemingway and Faux Faulkner competitions, which include "The Old Man and the Flea" and "Abe's Saloon! Abe's Saloon!", maybe someone has.

HUMMING (TO ITSELF?)

All this brings us to a crucial lemma. Inasmuch as text-slotters and text-synthesizers have been around for decades, in the remainder of this book I focus entirely on computer writers of the third order – or, if you prefer, on computhors proper. The distinction is essential in that it rectifies the snag inherent in Lem's approach to the subject. Given that his scenario pertains exclusively to third-order computer writing, he is wrong to invoke indirect authorship at this level of creativity.

It is understandable why Lem would feel compelled to embrace both parts of his definition, even though at the deeper level they are at each other's throats. On its own, the first stipulation – which assigns authorship solely to the end-producer of a piece of writing – does a mouse-poor job of defining the causal chain of command. In this view, given that *From Literature to Biterature* was created as a computer file, the computer *is* its real author. This is no different from replaying one of Garry Kasparov's classic chess games from the transcript and claiming the victory for yourself.

Suppose, however, that one day you visit my study where you espy an odd-looking gizmo quietly humming (to itself?). As you enter, it bids you wait a few moments: the host is on his way. Soon thereafter the humming stops, and the machine begins to rain out pages of what, on inspection, turns out to be an original novel. I think I can guess your reaction to this state of affairs. Taking me for a practical joker, you will surmise that I had rigged a voice synthesizer to bid you welcome and by remote control entered the PRINT command a few seconds after your arrival.

This is what in the present environment everyone in his right mind should surmise had happened, rather than jump to the conclusion that they witnessed a spontaneous act of creation. But what if I did not enter any commands? What if I am as befuddled as you are? What if the novel turns out to be something I could not have written? These questions help identify the conditions for third-order biterary creation. Providing we can be sure that the situation is indeed the way I just delineated, we might be – though perhaps reluctantly – inclined to accept computhorship as a fact of life.

Our little scenario highlights a factor critical to computer authorship. The *differentia specifica* of computers capable of biterary creation lies not so much in the quality of the composition but in causal independence. Uncaused by underlying program or programmer, third-order creativity is *spontaneous*, changing the rules of the game at a stroke (and forever changing the meaning of the phrase "ghost-writing").

2

Computhors

Poetic Licence; Devotchka; Analytical Engine; EZ-Writer;
Möbius-Like; JFK; One-Armed Bandit; Homeostat Sapiens;
As It Sees Fit; Brainstorm; A1, B2, C3; Black Boxes

POETIC LICENCE

Here is how Lem envisions the circumstances surrounding the birth of third-order computhorship:

> The relaxational output of machines was first observed and recorded almost thirty years ago. It turned out to be a purely technical necessity that the prototypes (beginning with the 15th binasty) should be provided with rest periods during which their activity did not come to a standstill but, deprived of programmed directives, manifested itself as a peculiar "mumble."[1]

If we subtract almost thirty years from the putative publication date of the story, the advent of sentient computers should have occurred in or around 1980, an incurably optimistic calculation by today's reckoning. But, whereas the writer of fiction can take refuge behind poetic licence, AI scientists cannot.

In a popular book of prognoses, *Mind Children* (1988), a robotics engineer, Hans Moravec, contended that by 2030 machines would attain human-level intelligence. Ten years later he pushed the date forward to mid-century, then dropped explicit references to the timeline altogether. In *The Age of Intelligent Machines* (1990), Ray Kurzweil, an equally wide-eyed prognosticator, gushed that systems capable of passing the Turing test would be manufactured around 2020. He then revised the sooth to 2029 before going wholly mum on the timeline.

Outside of generating tabloid headlines, futuristic tasseography of this sort proves only that intelligent thinking is as hard to come by in humans as in machines. Unfazed, in 1997 the organizers of the RoboCup went public with another grandiose forecast. By mid-twenty-first century, they boasted, a team of autonomous robo-footballers would outplay the winners of the latest World Cup. As a marketing ploy, it worked: in 2004 the robotic Japan Open attracted a 150,000 spectators (all human).

In the midst of prognostic hype, it is easy to overlook that a computing revolution did take place at the time prophesied by Lem, even if it had nothing to do with his scenario. Remember: when "A History of Bitic Literature" was being written, computers filled small rooms, necessitated round-the-clock air-conditioning, and cost an arm and a leg – and a torso. Experts envisioned that the decrease in costs would be offset by the rise in capabilities, with the result that these expensive giants would remain relatively few. In the early 1950s the chairman of IBM was dumbfounded to have received more orders for the 701 mainframe than the five he had thought the market would bear.

With hindsight, he got the core idea right, albeit with a delay of about half a century. Cloud computing is currently exploiting a similar business model whereby remote end-users rent access time to run programs on costly and, consequently, comparatively few batteries of mainframes. But back in the summer of 1981, in a watershed in micro-computing, the launch of IBM's first desktop system nudged the industry precisely in the opposite direction.

While International Business Machines was not the first to manufacture a personal computer, its 5150 laid down the standard for desktops ever since. A triumph of miniaturization, it tipped the scales at a svelte thirty pounds when outfitted with two 5.25-inch diskette drives, forty kilobytes of built-in ROM, and a standard sixteen kilobytes (expandable to 256K) of user memory. Best of all, it sold for only $3,000, or a little above $7,000 in today's inflated currency.

DEVOTCHKA

Back to Lem's history of the future past. The first work of bitic literature to achieve world renown was *The Girl* (*Devotchka*) by a computhor known as Pseudodostoyevsky:

In the early 1950s the chairman of IBM was dumbfounded to have received more orders for the 701 mainframe than the five he had thought the market would bear.

It was composed during a phase of relaxation by a multimember aggregate whose assignment was to translate into English the collected works of the Russian writer. In his memoirs the distinguished scholar John Raleigh describes the shock he experienced upon receiving the Russian typescript of a composition signed with what he took to be the singular pseudonym of HYXOS. The impression which the work created on this Dostoyevsky expert must have been truly indescribable in its intensity, if, as he admits, he doubted whether he was in a conscious state! The authenticity of the work was for him beyond a doubt, although he knew Dostoyevsky had not written such a novel.[2]

It is not difficult to see how the initial reaction to creative computers could be one of dismay, incredulity, or even shock. Some Californians may have experienced the same gamut of emotions at the 1997 world premiere of Mozart's 42nd Symphony, more than two centuries after Wolfgang Amadeus began, ahem, decomposing. This time around, however, the unknown score had not been exhumed in someone's musty Viennese attic. It had been freshly minted by a computer algorithm in imitation of the master.

The principle is analogous to that employed by algorithms that could imitate human writers. Clever mathematical functions that hum at the heart of David Cope's by-now famous program EMI – Experiments in Musical Intelligence – begin by breaking down existing works into musical phrases. In the second phase, they synthesize novel compositions in the style of the original by using combinatorial variations on the input fortified with a musical grammar and syntax written by the programmer.

Mozart to Scott Joplin, opera to ragtime chop, the computer remasters the masters to ringing applause from human audiences that include cognitive scientists, music lovers, or even, in Douglas Hofstadter, both at once.

ANALYTICAL ENGINE

Time to unpack the concept of third-order computhorship. The logical place to start is with the first programmable computing machine. The term "machine" is doubly apt in this context since, by design, Charles Babbage's Analytical Engine was to work along mechanical rather than electrical lines. Babbage's first crack at a gearbox computer was the Difference Engine (completed after his death by his son Henry). The Analytical Engine preoccupied him on and off between 1833 and 1871, although it was never finished.

We owe a comprehensive account of this pioneering number-cruncher to Babbage's lifelong assistant, Augusta Ada, daughter of Lord Byron. Better known as Lady Lovelace, she was in all but name the world's first computer programmer. Her memoirs, which amount to a treatise on what today we would call software engineering, make clear that the Analytical Engine was to run along structural and functional lines analogous to modern processors.

In the midst of her discussion, however, she takes pains to underscore that the "Analytical Engine has no pretensions to *originate* anything. It can do *whatever we know how to order it to perform.*"[3] Indeed, in the century and a half since, Lovelace's remarks have come to typify one of the most persistent objections to Artificial Intelligence. The nay-sayers deny that computers might ever be able to accomplish things that are original, surprising, novel – things like writing an original novel.

On closer inspection, however, the objection leaks water worse than a colander in the galley on the Titanic. Like Lem, Lovelace triggers a conceptual meltdown when she conflates two discrete, although superficially related, concepts. The first is a *process*, delineated by the verb "to originate." The other is a *quality*, denoted by the adjective "original." The process entails volition and agency. The quality does not. The difference is critical: you can originate a potboiler without making it in any way original.

Lovelace is right to point out that computers as we know them are not capable of originating anything. But she is wrong to suggest that their output cannot amount to anything original – that it can never surprise. Think about it. If we could fully anticipate the results of all computations, there would be no point in running them in the first place. By default, computers generate fresh data. For all that, a sceptic might remain unimpressed by machines that deliver even the most startling or even counterintuitive results. Given that at bottom all this is a matter of juggling of ones and zeros, presumably we could do the job ourselves, right?

Could we? Today's molecular or DNA computers tackle problems so gnarly that even Titan or Tianhe-1A could not hope to crack them before our sun flames out into a red dwarf. Does the inconvenience or full-blown inability to replicate the computer's calculations by hand amount to its being original? Or do we move the goal post and redefine originality more selectively, say, by removing it into the realm of art? Creative intentions, symbolic expression, or aesthetic nuance are frequently afforded the status of a Maginot Line that machines could never cross.

If you happen to think so, think again. Complex compositions admired by connoisseurs for their Beethoven, Brahms, Chopin, Mahler, or Rachmaninoff-like qualities have already been executed by tone-deaf polynomial functions. Paintings generated by mindless circuitry have been exhibited in London's Tate Modern, Amsterdam's Stedelijk Museum, the Brooklyn Museum, and the San Francisco Museum of Modern Art. Critical appreciations have been written about prose generated by populations of binary pulses racing in and out of logic gates.

EZ-WRITER

For all that, Lovelace's stipulation does furnish a good approxima-
tion of third-order computhorship. First-order text compilers and
second-order text synthesizers, no matter how clever or even original, cannot *originate* anything. In contrast, third-order computer
writers should be capable of acts of literary composition in and of
themselves – acts that are *spontaneous*, i.e., causally independent.

In practice, it must be said, the distinction may turn out to be
more blurry and gradualistic than this cut-and-dried picture suggests. Suppose you issue a request to a state-of-the-art synthesizer of
the EZ-Writer variety: "Write me a crime thriller." Suppose it does
so. The plot is generic, but then you did not ask for an existential
psychodrama. On the plus side, mixed in with the narrative fodder,
you find a few unconventional twists, an abundance of forensic
lore, decent enough characterization, and even a couple of seemingly self-reflexive passages on computers' potential in solving real-
life cases and plotting crime thrillers.

By all accounts, you get an ably executed potboiler of the quality that would not stand out from a rack of paperbacks that garnish
Costco or Wal-Mart checkout counters. Would you not be inclined
to allow, then, that the ostensibly second-order computer *created*
this crime thriller? Wouldn't your original request be essentially of
the same order as Little, Brown's commissioning Mailer, for a fee,
to write a book about NASA and the Apollo 11 moonshot?

Is it the fact that, unlike Mailer, the machine would not get paid
for its labours that might prevent us from acknowledging an act
of literary creation? Is it the fact that it apparently could not disobey the command? Or that, in the absence of your request, you
could be confident that the computer would not execute anything, whereas you could not rule out the possibility that Mailer
might still have penned *Of a Fire on the Moon* even if no one paid
him?

Right or wrong, I think some of us might be inclined to accept
that the semantic and aesthetic open-endedness of the request to
write a mystery thriller would satisfy the condition of independent
creation. But how about originating something decidedly unorigi-
nal? Suppose every time you ask the computer to write a crime
thriller, it produces a marginally different variation on the first, just

Suppose you issue a request to a state-of-the-art synthesizer of the EZ-Writer variety: "Write me a crime thriller." Suppose it does so.

as human hacks do. How do criteria of originality affect the criteria of origination?

Although, as I documented in *From Lowbrow to Nobrow* (2005), *every* novel is an amalgam of invention and convention, the machine's repetitiveness would be sure to raise doubts about its creative independence, notwithstanding the merits of the original composition. The bar is, as always, lower for humans. Dan Brown recycles clichés at a rate that ought to win him accolades from Greenpeace with seemingly no fear of being exposed as a mindless automaton.

Originality is inherently contextual and comparative, being contingent on the quality and degree of imitation and innovation. Even so, the connection between computhors and biterature is bound to be inversely proportional. The less control the writer

exerts over the execution of the work, the more we may hesitate
before attributing authorship. But what counts as executing a biterary work spontaneously, i.e., without consequential human
input? And what counts as consequential in the first place?

MÖBIUS-LIKE

Patterns have remarkable causal powers. Right now, the patterns
inscribed on this page cause you to flex your muscles so as to hold
a bound sheaf of pages in your hands, to adjust your posture so
your eyes can scan the print, to pause the scan when your physical
resources flag, and so on. Inside your head, they precipitate variations in the intensity with which hemoglobin oxygenates your brain
and, deeper still, variations in the firings of your neurons.

On a more holistic level, my patterns of thoughts inscribed in
patterns of alphabetical whorls may fire up your imagination so
much that you will skip dinner to continue reading, or they may
tire you out and make you skip a few pages. At a later date, they
may cause you to write a book review, write your own book of patterns, change the way you think about things, or even change your
life in general, as some books have done for some readers.

As you may have noticed, I tried in the course of the last two
paragraphs to separate (physical) effects from (mental) affects. If
this is not as easy as it sounds, it is because these two levels twine
with and feed back into each other, Möbius-like. Both accurately
describe the causal potency of patterns. Both are equally valid. But
only one of them is of direct interest to us as conscious beings, not
least because it is the only level of which we are conscious.

Needless to say, it is not the level of myocardial peristalses,
amino-acid bonding, falling synaptic dominos, or molecular elec-
tron-shedding. It is the level of intentions, beliefs, and desires – the
level of making plans, of experiencing confusions, of making
errors and becoming aware of having made them, and such like.
The type of mental activity that concerns us resides, in other words,
on the macro level of minds, these more or less coherent collec-
tions of mental processes that combine into the inwardly experienced "I."

And needless to say, mental macro states are at bottom equivalent to neurological events. Intensely subjective experiences of external or internal stimuli, be it a predator leaping out of bushes or

the grief of a "Dear John letter," are nothing more than synapses tickling neighbouring synapses in the right way. Only, they are not registered as staccatos of neural discharges but as patterns of mental events. Not coincidentally, this is also the standard level of analysis of causation in the human sciences – the level of analysis at which explanations are considered to be adequate.

JFK

At the macro level of instrumental causes and psychosocial motivations, we look to identify forces and factors that produce a certain effect in the given circumstances. The standard level of analysis acts as a stopping rule in our search for explanations, telling us in effect when they are sufficiently deep. A stopping rule is essential insofar as explanations can be refined without end, going from the level of intentions to the level of muscular exertions, hemoglobin oxygenation, firing neurons, or even electrical, molecular, and quantum events.

Suppose you are tasked with giving a full account of Kennedy's death in Dallas in November 1963. Unlike Jim Garrison, you are given access to all the evidence unavailable to the prosecutor, including the president's brain, the suit of clothes, the unwashed limousine, the chief pathologist's unburned autopsy notes – the lot. JFK died, you conclude at the end of your exhaustive travails, because multiple rifle shots fired from several directions fatally damaged his vital organs.

You consider your job well done. Your findings meet the standards of forensic investigations of homicide by firearm by specifying the direct causes sufficient to bring the result in question. But did your inquiry really establish how the president of the United States could have been assassinated or why he was shot in the first place? Judging by the generations of Americans who dismiss the Warren Report as an elaborate cover-up, the answer is "No." Your explanation may be *accurate* without being *adequate*.

The difference lies in causal depth. A cause is too shallow to explain why an effect occurred if it is just one of the ways in which another cause, as intimately connected with the effect, produced the effect in question. The true account of the factors behind JFK's death: "Snipers' bullets fatally damaged his vital organs," demonstrates why this is so. The report is accurate but inadequate – the mechanism it identifies is causally true but unsatisfying because too shallow.

Looking for causes, we need to isolate the effective mechanisms of change rather than ones that may be only superficially linked to the effects. There are two ways in which superficial causes can undermine the effect of underlying ones. In *Fact and Method* (1987), Richard Miller calls them "depth as necessity" and "depth as priority." A causal agent (C) helping to bring about a wished-for effect (W) is too shallow to explain why (W) has occurred if a hidden cause (H) undermines (C) in either of the following two ways:

- depth as necessity: if (C) had not been present, (W) would have come about anyway.
- b) depth as priority: (H) is an antecedent cause of (C), which in turn causes (W), yet (H) is too intimately linked to (C) to be left outside a valid causal account.

ONE-ARMED BANDIT

Let us flesh out these abstractions with reference to the computer world. If (C)omputer had not been present, biterary (W)ork would have come about anyway since (H)uman agent would have used a substitute for (C)omputer to bring the same result. For closed forms, any randomizing device could replace the machine, demonstrating that the latter is inessential to the creative process. Conclusion? First-order compilers fail "depth as necessity" insofar as they are causally undermined. The computer is merely a mediating and thus dispensable tool in the hands of the programmer.

Now "depth as priority." (H)uman is an antecedent cause to (C)omputer, which in turn produces biterary (W)ork, yet (H)uman is too intimately linked to (C)omputer to be bracketed off. Our interest here is not with first-order writing, which falls under "depth as necessity" but with open forms. Could a work have come into existence in essentially the same form without the human agent? Or was the programmer essential to the generation of the work in the given manner? If the latter, we are looking at second-order computer writing.

The causal account makes the concept of computhorship a little more precise. We have identified two ways in which the genesis of a biterary work can be undermined by accompanying or antecedent factors. Both narrow down what is acceptable as genuine, i.e., spontaneous biterary creativity. There must be a direct and not underlying causal link between a computhor and the work in its given shape for the machine to be its genuine author.

Naturally, current socio-cultural norms for linking artists to their works do not recognize machines as intentional agents. This makes it inevitable that, looking at "depth as priority," we will always search upstream for evidence of human agency. So long as there is no question of intentionality, and thus of potentially balking at commands, the situation is unproblematic. The bylines and royalties remain safely in our hands. The converse would be analogous to being denied the jackpot from a one-armed-bandit in Vegas by virtue of the argument that you *only* pulled the handle, whereas the machine executed the steps necessary to produce the torrent of quarters.

HOMEOSTAT SAPIENS

Third-order computhors are defined by spontaneous, i.e., causally independent, creativity. Causal independence cannot, naturally, be divorced from a capacity for independent thinking. Thinking, in turn, presupposes homeostatic response to the ambient world. In general, survival-oriented behaviour comes in two types. The first is instinctual (genotypic). It depends on a palette of hard-wired responses that guarantee swift and reliable action in the face of commonplace environmental stimuli.

Whether you like it or not, clear and present danger will kickstart your sympathetic nervous system: pupils dilating, heart pumping, blood vessels widening, adrenalin rushing, glucose ready to burn rubber in flight or fight, all systems primed to respond to the source of anxiety or panic. Instincts may yet become programmable into machines, but let's face it: amoebas do not write novels. By definition, biterary computhors point us toward a different type of homeostasis altogether.

The learning homeostat, which organizes its behaviour on the basis of historically acquired knowledge, has obvious drawbacks: it is slow, indecisive, and error prone. What it offers on the positive side of the ledger is, above all, foresight. Inductive reasoning can generate inferences about the future, which can then be averted or cultivated instead of only responded to. With foresight comes flexibility, which throws the doors open to a spectrum of behaviours that dwarfs anything preset by evolution.

In reality, it is hard to find either type in pure form. Even thoughtless bacteria "learn" to cope with environmental hazards, albeit in an elemental fashion, gaining proactive protection from reactive survival. At the other end of the scale, *Homo sapiens* is also an amalgam of both. At each point in development, the human mind is a composite of information from genetic endowment – which can come into play during specific phases of ontogeny, such as the onset of Theory of Mind around nine to twelve months old – as well as formal and informal (inductive, analogical, emotional) experience.

Already at birth, babies are equipped with instinctive responses such as crying, suckling, evacuating digestive waste, parental bonding, and so on. Even so, their long-term survival requires a protracted process of development and learning. What a contrast to the overwhelming majority of terrestrial fauna who are ready to fend for themselves from the moment they step off the biological assembly line.

Among higher animals, however, learning also plays a critical role. To take but one example, birds like oyster-catchers take years to master the technique of opening bivalves. Some rely on brute force, hammering their way in. Others hunt in shallow tidal waters, on the lookout for morsels that have not yet closed their shells. Still others pick up unattached shells, carry them away from the flock so as not to attract attention, and proceed to cut the oyster along the hinge. In each case, they learn the particular method from their parents.

AS IT SEES FIT

We are unlike stored-program machines in one fundamental way: we *learn*. We can override – i.e., unlearn – established patterns of response, including those related to the learning process itself. In *Consciousness Explained* (1991) Daniel Dennett coined the expression "postnatal design-fixing" to describe not only what we normally understand by learning but also normal ontogenetic development in people, mammals, or birds. Taking cue, let me generalize what is essential about learning while bypassing the differences between carbon and silicon (or graphene or whatever non-silicon chips will be made of).

Learning is the capacity to transform internal states and external actions in response to incoming data, and to evaluate performance and correlate future actions to improvement in performance. A Japanese sensorized toilet bowl has an array of feedbacks to detect variations in its environment which it counters by adjusting the seat temperature, playing music of your choice, perfuming the air, flushing water, bidding you a good day, and what not. But intricate as it is, the system is incapable of scoring its operations and rewriting its input-output algorithm. In short, it is incapable of learning.

In contrast, the rule-book of any learning algorithm is not time invariant. A computer that goes to school must be able to rewrite its code. An early program that put this point in perspective was the mathematical explorer AM. Preloaded with knowledge of set theory, two hundred heuristics, and a handful of meta-level search principles, it was rolled out in the 1970s as a brand new tool for generating new mathematical concepts and conjectures. Yet, after a few initial triumphs, it became clear that its efficacy was, in fact, quite limited.

AM's usefulness turned out to be inversely proportional to the time it was allowed to run, simply because, as its conjectures grew, it was unable to alter its heuristics. Remember: at its most basic level, learning is an ability to acquire information and feed it back into one's behaviour – including the learning process itself. Recognizing AM's problem, David Peat recommended in *Artificial Intelligence* (1988), "An obvious improvement therefore would be to have it modify its heuristics as it learns."[4]

These lessons are not lost on the current crop of programmers. One of the most talked-about developments in higher-level heuristics is layered search – essentially a meta-level heuristic whereby the very framework within which the search is conducted is subject to modification. Once again, the implications are staggeringly simple and simply staggering. A learning machine ought to be able to rewrite its program *as it sees fit* in the course of its operations. Learning bootstraps any system's capacity to learn, i.e., to become capable of interacting with the environment by means of historically acquired world knowledge and evaluating such interaction.

BRAINSTORM

The capacity to evaluate one's own cognitive, conative, and affective states both at the ground level and at the meta level is a must

A Japanese sensorized toilet bowl has an array of feedbacks to detect variations in its environment which it counters by adjusting the seat temperature,
playing music of your choice, perfuming the air, flushing water, bidding you
a good day, and what not. But intricate as it is, the system is incapable of
scoring its operations and rewriting its input-output algorithm. In short, it is
incapable of learning.

for any learning system. Yet even this seemingly straightforward
principle can go awry, as it did in one expert program in the early
1980s. Douglas Lenat's EURISKO was created to gather data, spot
regularities, and formulate domain hypotheses, while simultane-
ously extending its knowledge representation. In plain English, the
program was to evaluate its own efficacy in problem solving with a
view to bettering its performance next time around.

Put differently, EURISKO followed two kinds of heuristics. Both
the ground level and the meta level directives were programmed
into it from the start. But the meta level heuristic also fed back into
itself, having been designed to evaluate ground level performance

and modify *itself* accordingly. Procedures, concepts, and rules of electronic thumb that proved useful in the execution of ground level tasks would be assigned a higher value for future operations.

All in a day's work, except that at one point the system got too smart for its own good, applying the rules in a manner completely unforeseen by the programmers. It all began when a heuristic made a minor discovery, at which point it routinely upgraded itself on the list of useful heuristics. Then it had a brainstorm. It took the fact that it had just made a discovery as a discovery in itself, so it awarded itself another pat on the back points-wise. Then it took *that* as another discovery, and gave itself more points, and so on ad infinitum! A new twist, in other words, on the old idea of self-programming intimated in John McCarthy's 1958 paper "Programs with Common Sense."

Like experimental rats that keep pressing the lever stimulating their pleasure centre to the total neglect of the need for food or drink, Lenat's expert found a loophole that permitted it to short-circuit back on itself, iterating this minimal cycle to the detriment of the analytic work it was supposed to do. The lesson? Homeostatic machines need some form of survival instinct, likely in the form of algedonic (pleasure-pain) control, to help them override siren calls when their very survival is at stake. Even survival instincts are, of course, susceptible to being overridden for the same reason that they are in lab rats or street junkies, hooked on stimuli whose intensity and ease of access surpass everything that evolution prepared them for.

Make no mistake: first things will always come first. Once it evolves something like common sense, the first thing any survival-minded machine will (and ought to) do is secure an independent power supply to make sure that it remains independent from external perturbations, such as our fickle goodwill. This is to say that, much as we modify our behaviour to our advantage when we learn something, learning computhors will modify their behaviour in ways that suits not us but *them*.

A1, B2, C3

What is the colour of a blue truck? Where is your nose when you're at home? What happens to an ice cube in a hot drink? How many feet do four cats have together? How is the father of Andy's moth-

er related to Andy? What does the letter M look like upside down?
What comes next after A1, B2, C3? These are only some of the self-
evident questions posed to computers over the past two decades in
annually contested Turing-like tests. The quality of responses has
been decidedly underwhelming.

After more than half a century, backed by tens of billions of
research dollars, the sharpest brains in the field have achieved practically nothing. Not one machine to date has managed to answer the
above banalities correctly, far less with an air of bored insouciance.
Long-time critics of the so-called Good Old-Fashioned Artificial
Intelligence who grew up with Hubert L. Dreyfus's *What Computers
Can't Do* (1972) and *What Computers Still Can't Do* (1979) can only
feel vindicated.

The chronic lack of achievement in top-down programming of
general problem-solving heuristics suggests that the traditional
approach is an alley blinder than the one into which Ray Charles
and Stevie Wonder might blunder on a tandem bike. It is high time
to admit it: the only way to computhors is bottom up, via computers that learn. And since learning is the capacity for self-redesign
on the basis of acquired knowledge, learning in the learning computer is going to be expectation driven, i.e., hypothesis forming.

The ability to anticipate developments as part of a proactive attitude to incoming data is the idea behind tomorrow's systems
already at work today. Whereas standard source-code has all even-
tualities preset in advance, neural networks have very few preset
values. At the heart of each connectionist system beats an algorithm that digests the input and spits out the output – *and* feeds
what is just did back into the algorithm.

Using human neuronal and axonal connections as templates,
neural nets already run chunks of the world today, sometimes
learning the tricks of the trade on the job. They read facial expressions for security agencies, wash and decode everyday-level speech
for spy satellites, identify and prioritize targets in battlefield conditions, tag fraudulent patterns in credit card purchases, pre-approve
credit for bankers, predict box-office take of Hollywood movies
and pop-chart climbers, monitor prison inmates, and, last but not
least, suggest purchases on Amazon or rentals on Netflix.

How do they do it? Deceptively simple: Monday net goes to
school on Sunday net goes to school on Saturday net goes to school
on Friday, and so on. Over time, incoming information builds con-

nections, determining their strength in relation to all other connections and weightings (strengths) thereof. Springing into existence, becoming the default, decreasing in importance, or completely atrophying as new input dominates the network, patterns of connections reflect not the net's original programming but how it evolved in the course of its operations.

BLACK BOXES

Learning computers will develop (reprogram themselves) in ways distinct from one another in response to different patterns of environmental pressures, sort of like monozygotic twins do as they grow up. This is true even today on the level of programming languages, which can precipitate different performances and, as such, different outputs. Naturally, all code can be emulated by other code. But it requires an awful lot of effort to make sure that not a single one or zero gets lost in translation.

This little fact of life has colossal ramifications for learning computers. With self-reprogramming at the heart of the learning process, serial-production machines are bound to diverge from one another until they acquire distinctly individual characteristics (not to say personalities). Ask two computhors the same question and, as with today's economists, you will get two answers. Thus, even if one could assume no "prenatal" differences in architecture and programming, "postnatal" differences will be a given in machines advanced enough to write biterature in and of themselves.

Does all this spell out l-o-s-s o-f c-o-n-t-r-o-l? Unquestionably. That was entailed already by the idea of machines rewriting their own code. But the learning computer will not stop with software. By necessity it will also begin to "rewrite" its hardware: plug in more chips, redesign existing chips, rewire connections among chips, replace chips with racemic colloids, link up with other chipless systems, and so on. We can see the future today when computers are used to design the circuitry of machines whose dimensions and complexity exceed human powers of integration.

Once they begin to reprogram and redesign themselves, computhors will effectively become black boxes in which it will be no longer possible to trace a direct line between input and output. This is to say that there will be propositions that the machine itself will not be able to explain how it arrived at, nor are we going to be in a position to retroactively find out. Ultimately, a self-programming computhor may change its configuration to the point where it will no longer even be or do what it was originally designed for.

This is assuming, of course, that it was designed for something in the first place. It is possible to envision machines, constructed on evolutionary principles, that are not designed for anything in particular, unless it is survival and, possibly, reproduction. All this would be consistent not only with Turing's vision of universal machines but with his prototypical design of the ACE computer which to a degree was capable of modifying its own instructions.

3

Bibliosophy

La Chanson de Roland; The Motherboard of All Problems;
Little Endian; Algo Trading; Father Roberto Busa; Riverside
Shakespeare; Death in Holbein; Zettabyte; A Hamlet Every Eight
Seconds; A Pill That Makes Me Feel Loved

LA CHANSON DE ROLAND

What will be the professional response from scholars and critical institutions to the rave new world in which literature is created by authors other than human? Lem envisages the appearance of two schools of biterary studies, each with a methodologically distinctive approach to computhor writing.

Largely ignoring the specificity of non-human intelligence, the traditionalists of the "business as usual" school fix their attention solely on the texts, ignoring the functional and architectural specifics of computer artists. In distinction, the multidisciplinarians favour a more comprehensive approach. Their tenet is that at least some facets of biterature become meaningful only in the light of the technical specifics of its creators. Lem brings out the singularity of the latter approach via reference to human writers where, for obvious reasons, such anatomical and functional factors are taken for granted, being common to all members of the species. In terms of romance philology, for example, it would be bizarre to characterize the anonymous author of *La Chanson de Roland* as a multicellular vertebrate, a mammal "which is viviparous, pneumobranchiate, placental, and the like."[1]

In computhors, on the other hand, variations in design are destined to impact the manner in which they experience the world, differentiating them not only from us but, equally, from one another. To take the simplest scenario, the world of a machine equipped with infrared sensors will be appreciably at odds with ours. Its nights will not be inscrutable or menacing. Its stock of symbols, similes, or synecdoches will not connote them with danger or death. Its poetry and prose will, in short, differ from ours in this respect, unless it deliberately alludes to our nighttime, still and Bible black.

The differences do not, of course, end there. While we are bounded by physics and biology, computers are not. There is nothing to prevent them from outfitting themselves with magnetic sensors like those in some marine species, quickening or retarding the internal clocks that would allow them to live on the scale of a fruit fly or a continent, interlacing at light speeds with peripherals scattered around the world, allowing them to be in effect everywhere at once – and who knows what else.

Even these extraordinary scenarios pale, however, next to what can be simulated inside a computer. There will be worlds inside worlds inside worlds, with arbitrary dimensions, evolving laws of nature, or, if you so choose, manna falling from heaven on every sabbath. There will be universes pan-psychic and Panglossian, governed by deities malevolent or kind, with fates predetermined or completely chaotic, and even universes in which existence will be coeval with the duration of the simulation – in other words, eternal.

THE MOTHERBOARD OF ALL PROBLEMS

On the face of it, Lem's division of future humanities seems plausible enough. Once again, however, it glosses over a mess of counter-examples that puts the whole schema under a cloud. For starters, the *reductio ad absurdum* of the biological traits of the author of *La Chanson de Roland* works only to the extent that it homes in on such an extreme example. Common critical practice gives, in fact, plenty of reason to question the tenets of biterary textualism.

Certain aspects of human literature do become salient and meaningful, after all, in the light of the anatomical and functional aspects of their creators. *The Narrative of the Life of Frederick Douglass* (1845) comes alive precisely because Douglass experiences and describes the world through the prism of his blackness. Helen Keller's deafness and blindness endow her autobiographies *The Story of My Life* (1903) and *The World I Live In* (1908) with an existential "vision" that is uniquely hers.

Whatever you may think of Women's Studies, Black Studies, Queer Studies, and cognate academic programs, they amply testify that a number of humanists focus their professional gaze precisely on the correlations between various anatomical and functional subclasses of the genus *Homo* and their cultural output. As I argued exhaustively in *Literature, Analytically Speaking*, state-of-the-art arguments in aesthetics demand, in fact, that interpreters take note of the identity of the author within the context of an artwork's creation.

Another problem for biterary traditionalists stems from the assumption that they can do away with references to computhor architecture. For this to be true, the latter would have to be generic enough not to be a factor in creation. On this assumption, two machines of the same type could only write one and the same (type of) novel. Obviously, nothing could be further from the truth. Causally independent computhors will only be generic in the same sense that human writers are. We are all viviparous, pneumo-branchiate, placental, and the like, but we are also all unique.

Remember the last time you used someone else's laptop? Customized to suit another person's preferences, it makes efficient navigation impossible. Everything in the wrong place, useful short-cuts and commands hidden from view, the idiosyncratic work habits of the owner stamped all over the screen – and this just for a custom, menu-driven job. By the time we get to computhors, they will have as much in common as not. Each will be a creative individual as distinct from one another as I am from you.

For practical reasons, therefore, biterary studies might need to take the multidisciplinary route, at least to the same extent that it is commonly taken in literary studies today. Extending critical inquiries to computhors' configuration and functionality would appear to be a *sine qua non* inasmuch as it may appreciably affect their artistic vision. Naturally, this is taking for granted that the technical parameters of the machine authors' hardware and software will remain transparent to our scrutiny. And herein lies the motherboard of all problems.

LITTLE ENDIAN

Admirable in ambition, the multidisciplinary approach may be a dead end from the start. Even in the last century, in the comparatively primitive days of number crunchers, hardware architecture

was a discipline so specialized that no critic could be expected
to be familiar with the nitty-gritty. Do terms such as WAW hazard,
Amdahl's Law, Little Endian mode, or block offset mean anything
to an average, or even above-average, literary critic? What about
more eccentric mouthfuls, such as adaptive channel queue routing
on k-ary n-cubes?

When was the last time you ran into a specialist in Renaissance
drama with expertise or, for that matter, interest in Black Widow
High-Radix Folded Clos Networks? How many tenured Shake-
speareans have a grip on techniques for mounting transistors on
integrated circuits? Deep UV lithography? High-k gate dielectrics?
Junction laser annealing? How many could even explain what a
transistor is? (An electrical switch with a source and drain for the
current to enter and leave, plus a channel – aka connector – with
a gate that switches on and off in response to variation in voltage.)

Problems with multidisciplinary methodology are further exac-
erbated by the task of finding a common language of exchange
among specialists from different areas. Is it even remotely likely
that large interdisciplinary teams will work out a method of vector-
ing their disparate levels of analysis on the way to a better understanding of biterary art? After all, this Herculean labour is still to
be carried out within the literary-critical camp itself, who cannot
even understand themselves let alone find a common language of
exchange with the public, to whom lit-crit remains as relevant as
Thomist scholasticism.

It is true that we need scientific literacy. The stakes for contemporary civilization are just too high. In democracies, even those as
sclerotic as in the West, the torrent of issues demanding a public
debate and thus a better-than-average scientific education swells by
the minute: cloning, euthanasia, stem cells, eco-wars, gene splicing,
sociobiology, spyware, tactical nukes, war-zone drones, cybercul-
ture, research ethics, budget priorities.

Unfortunately, scientific literacy is an oxymoron in more senses
than one. Information explosion is a fact of life, and research agencies' calls for Renaissance thinkers who would speak the Babel of
languages of the arts *and* the balkanizing multiplex of the sciences
amount to calls for a utopia. And these chronic difficulties are only
destined to grow more acute when it comes to accounting for the
nuts and bolts of auto-evolving machines of the future.

For the race will not stop there. Unconstrained by biology, evolution in thinking computers will advance much faster than we can imagine – certainly faster than anyone's ability to puzzle out or even track their internal architecture. In the end, future scholars committed to critically linking biterature to the structural and functional specs of their creators are simply condemned to fall more and more behind as the pace of self-redesign accelerates beyond what is humanly comprehensible.

ALGO TRADING

Another factor guaranteed to seal computhors off not only from humanist but from human inquiry is software transparency. Even more so than on the level of hardware, today's source code is breeding the first generation of black-box computers. Prima facie, it might seem that no such project could ever get off the ground. The same anxiety that prompts authorities worldwide to want to regulate the Internet would rally all against the idea of computer autonomy via code opacity.

The naive assumption is that the decision to okay the development of non-transparent applications remains in our hands. It does not. As early as 1976, in *Computer Power and Human Reason*, Joseph Weizenbaum warned that many of the massive software aggregates of his day were slowly disappearing in the cloud of superhuman complexity. Subsequent scientists, who did not necessarily share his sense of alarm, were more than ready to concede, nevertheless, that the dimensions of contemporary code were edging toward the brink of incomprehension.

In *The Creative Computer* (1984), Donald Michie and Rory Johnston argued that unless the operating systems of the 1990s were tailored to fit the human window, they would become too complex and opaque to control. Their red flags fell on deaf ears (blind eyes, really), and the 1990s gave every Windows user a lesson on what can happen when even everyday PC operating code becomes too complicated to debug. Glitches that would as soon crash the system as freeze it till kingdom come became commonplace enough to spawn a library of Zen-like haikus mocking the world according to Bill Gates:

Chaos reigns within.
Reflect, repent, and reboot.
Order shall return.

Fearing that bigger and bigger chunks of the source code were slipping out of human hands, Michie and Johnston argued that, between efficiency and inscrutability, "performance must be sacrificed for the sake of transparency."[2] The metaphorical opening of the human window, they insisted, should optimize the interface between people and machines by creating an online environment sensitive to the needs of the former and not the latter. A beautiful vision, if you like fairy tales.

The reality is more Grimm than Disney. Among today's specialists, it is pretty much taken for granted that oversight of computer code is about to slip out of our hands. We rely on software, moaned one whiz in 2011, "that we can no longer read."[3] Just in case you might be ready to dismiss this plaint in complacence, remember that at least half of Wall Street trading is in the hands of algorithms. They monitor traffic in shares and commodities and, when stocks hit a critical value, automatically kick into action, buying, selling, and burying millions of small-time investors in their wake.

Algo-trading, as it is called in the business, underpins *all* rapid-fire trades, called officially HFT (high-frequency trading) but better known on the floor as "sniping" – not to mention "sniffing" (trend-spotting), "spoofing" (pretend buying), and other arcane forms of wealth management by digital computers. Stocks worth billions of dollars are acquired or flushed in a heartbeat by inert binary code. With HFT making up almost three-quarters of all share trading in the United States, more than a few brokerage companies have already installed artificial intelligence systems that can adapt floor strategies of their own accord.

Historically, investors have always raced against time. Nathan Rothschild is said to have made a fortune when he scooped Napoleon's defeat at Waterloo by means of a carrier pigeon. The multibillion-dollar Internet sea cable between Singapore and Tokyo that is currently being laid will shave as much as three seconds on the entire journey. Think this is nothing? In the time it takes you to think that, HFT algo traders can complete a million separate trades.

The Pentagon still fights wars, but it can no longer coordinate them without an army of sophisticated algorithms that look after the logistics, run autonomous surveillance, calculate all firing formulas, and even determine frontline units' combat-worthiness and thus, indirectly, who is going to catch bullets. The whole planet is

Just in case you might be ready to dismiss this plaint in complacence, remember that at least half of Wall Street trading is in the hands of algorithms.

critically dependent on information supplied by Internet search engines whose reliability and accuracy is simply taken on faith.

Google search engines put millions of web pages at your fingertips in milliseconds, creating a potent illusion of better access to the information out yonder in cyberspace. The fact is, however, that you will never be in a position to inspect even a tiny fraction of this embarrassment of riches, nor monitor the algorithm's search priorities. The blind code calls for blind faith from end-users, a quaint notion in view of docketfuls of lawsuits filed against Google for fixing search results.

Is Wall Street more religion than economic science? Perhaps, given the in-house name for these semi-autonomous traders: black-box algorithms, codes that no one, even in principle, is capable of bringing to heel. Not that there is any sinister design on anyone's part. Perish the thought of electronic overlords poised to take control. All we are seeing is a marriage of convenience between human nature and the code's ability to integrate colossal fields of data – and to integrate the integrations.

FATHER ROBERTO BUSA

The obstacles looming before Lem's multidisciplinary teams of students and professors of biterature appear to be insuperable. Insofar as computer code and architecture are doomed to become species of black apps and black ops, even the largest multidisciplinary teams that departments of biterature could assemble will be of no avail. Black-box computhors are by definition closed to analysis, whether on the level of builtware or bitware.

The causal link between computer anatomy and its output, necessary to validate multidisciplinary studies of biterature, will have been erased forever. Seen in this light, the future of departments of biterature ought to belong to the traditionalists of the business-as-usual (or rather, business-as-unusual) school. Oddly enough, examples of humanists turning to machines for help in dealing with the intricacies of art and culture go back to the dawn of the computer age.

One of the earliest of such computer-powered projects dates all the way back to 1949. That same year the EDSAC, the first practical stored-program machine, smashed all speed records by executing more than seven *hundred* operations per second. Meanwhile, in Italy,

Father Roberto Busa – Jesuit, linguist, and computer maven – set out to compile a comprehensive word index and concordance to the collected works of Thomas Aquinas. The undertaking enjoyed the blessing of his superiors, more than glad to yoke the power of the computer to the name to the Lord.

Their enlightened stance is hardly an ecclesiastical anomaly, at least when it comes to binary code. Giving the lie to the facile opposition between religion and science, Pope Benedict XVI, for example, endorsed the Internet as truly blessed, going as far as to spread the gospel on Twitter. All the same, back in 1949 Father Busa's mission was nothing short of monumental. The entire Thomist corpus amounts to the length of ten complete editions of Shakespeare – nine million words in toto (which still pales next to English Wikipedia's 2.5 billion).

In a foretaste of the scale of the project, Busa had previously compiled 10,000 index cards by hand just for the inventory of the preposition "in," which he considered philosophically significant. In the end, it took him two years of programming before he could even begin to transfer text to punch cards, the state-of-the-art data-storage devices of the time. Unsurprisingly, the first volume of his life's work did not appear till 1973, while the whole project took a better part of half a century to complete. (Father Busa himself passed away in 2011 at the age of ninety-seven.) Today, his magnum opus fits on seventy thousand pages in fifty-six volumes or, in the sign of the times, on a single low-density disk.

RIVERSIDE SHAKESPEARE

The earliest complete concordance, with all words accounted for, was, as you may have guessed, *A Complete and Systematic Concordance of the Works of Shakespeare*. It filled nine volumes, the first appearing in 1968 and the last in 1980, and became the basis for the *Riverside Shakespeare*, at that time the compleatest set of the bard's plays and poems, fortified by learned footnotes on Elizabethan life and theatre. Printed on super-thin vellum-like paper, this portable – well, luggable – edition weighed in at under three kilos.

In most cases a concordance is only the first step on the way to textual analysis, and it was no different with Shakespeare. In one of the simplest applications, the database was first used to quantify the richness of language by correlating word-types with word-

Unsurprisingly, the first volume of Busa's life's work did not appear till 1973, while the whole project took a better part of half a century to complete. (Father Busa himself passed away in 2011 at the age of ninety-seven.)

tokens. To no one's surprise, it verified that England's national poet possessed the most extensive and sophisticated verbal resources of all time. An unparalleled neologist, among many other things, he brought phrases such as "a foregone conclusion" (*Othello*) into daily English. In a more advanced mode, the concordance was harnessed to map the intensity of certain themes by tracking operational word frequencies.

But the true bombshell came with the plays. Traditionally, Shakespeare's plays have been divided into four genres: comedies (*As You Like It*), histories (*King Henry V*), tragedies (*Hamlet*), and tragicomedies or romances (*The Tempest*). Using relative frequencies of linguistic events, experts set out to test the accuracy of this classification.

The results for the most part corroborated their expectations, with the computer labelling thirty-five of the thirty-eight plays in accordance with the canon. There were, however, three exceptions, the most notable being the odd placement of *King Henry IV, Part 2*. Conventionally tagged as – what else? – a history, in the computer's opinion it was a comedy. And its rationale was hard to argue with. In the play, Falstaff, the scallywag adviser to the young monarch and one of the greatest comic creations in history, literally steals the show by speaking more than half of the lines.

Another triumph of traditional literary analysis aided by the computer was the resolution of authorship of a batch of Federalist papers, a series of essays written in 1787–88 on republican government and the proposed American Constitution. By external evidence, the papers were attributable either to Madison or Hamilton, but there the historians ran into a brick wall. To smash through it, the machine was asked to perform a frequency analysis of grammatical units (connectives, prepositions, etc.) typical of the two founding fathers. The results were spectacular, with the odds in favour of Madison being the author more than ten thousand times higher than for Hamilton

Computers are not, it should be stressed, a universal panacea for gaps in our knowledge. The Federalist paternity suit was resolved largely because there were only two alternatives, because the search space was limited, and because the literary analysts were trained in statistics and computers. All the same, over the years computer-driven stylistic analysis has been successfully applied to the detection of forgery – or, conversely, to the authentication – of wills, confessions, and other types of forensically sensitive documents.

DEATH IN HOLBEIN

One of the unhailed success stories of 1998 was a British interdisciplinary study of the extant versions of Chaucer's "The Wife of Bath" from *The Canterbury Tales*. The investigation, unique of its kind, was a milestone in literary studies. Using computing techniques developed originally for evolutionary biologists, a team of literary scholars, computer scientists, and biochemists restored the portrayal of the Wife of Bath from the various preserved scripts to what, it is believed, Chaucer had intended.

Impressive as this and other cases are, they are still worlds apart from the future in which computer writers are authors of literary works, rather than mere tools in their analysis. But even today algorithms are fast closing the gap between formalism and aesthetics –

between merely differentiating artistic techniques and making reliable aesthetic judgments. To be sure, machines are not yet pausing in contemplation of death in Holbein. But they are comfortably outdoing art connoisseurs in domains previously thought to be exclusively reserved for humans.

The principle is akin to that employed by the melody-spinning EMI. The computer samples an array of paintings and quantifies their visual and statistical aspects according to literally thousands of parameters: symmetry, texture, colour intensity, fractality, catastrophic (*pace* catastrophe theory) changes, and so on. At the end of this, it can not only unerringly identify the paintmanship but suggest unexpected aesthetic affinities, such as between Van Gogh and Pollock – closer than those between Van Gogh and his contemporaries Monet and Renoir, as held by conventional art criticism.

The next step is to produce an algorithm that will produce canvases in Van Gogh's or Pollock's style. In time, imitations will become impossible to tell from the originals, so much so that cunning Sotheby dealers will begin to sell them as such to drum up their value (they were preserved, they will say, in a potato barn crammed with paintings, as in *Bluebeard*, Kurt Vonnegut's novel about an abstract expressionist). The final step will be taken when the algorithm offers the dealers a take-it-or-leave-it split on as yet unpainted paintings.

We cannot leave the subject of computer-art attribution without a story that has a distinctly Lemian ring to it, even though it does not involve him in any way. The background is Lem's hometown of Cracow, and the setting is the historical Jagiellonian University where Lem taught literature and philosophy in the 1970s – or, as the story goes, the university's Institute of Science and Technology.

It was at the Institute that – according to an announcement made in 1980, a full four years before Racter – a software called Melpomene composed a novel called *Bagabone, Hem 'I Die Now*. The adventure story, set in the South Pacific and in Pidgin English, was described by the publicist as having been written by an EZ-Writer text synthesizer pre-programmed with Joyce, D.H. Lawrence, Britain's "angry young" writers from the 1950s, several women writers, and more than five thousand "semantic units" (whatever that means) of English, Pidgin English, and French. A nice story, except that, as soon became clear, there never was such software, just as in reality there never was any Institute of Science and Technology at the Jagiellonian University. The recipient of the royalties from this vanity-published book, identified only as G.E. Hughes, had perpetrated a hoax.

Bagabone was viewed with suspicion virtually from Day 1. Stuttering syntax and wonky semantics notwithstanding, its plot and character integrity implied such prodigious feats of processing as would be unattainable in funds-starved, strike-torn, Solidarity-era Poland. Pointedly, however, today the novel would likely be accepted at face value with hardly a demur. Indeed, as Turing implied in his ground-breaking paper, instead of resolving controversies head-on, the march of science and technology often dissolves them in a roundabout way by making them so commonplace as not to be worth a second thought.

ZETTABYTE

With the seemingly insurmountable obstacles blocking the pathway of biterary interdisciplinarians, the future seems to belong to scholars of the traditionalist school. Only there may not be much of a future either for the traditionalists or the multidisciplinarians. Forget for the moment the inscrutability of bitware and builtware, and face the biggest problem of the information age: what will happen if the sheer *quantity* of biterature exceeds our entire civilizational bandwidth?

Even today, the volume of the printed word alone is beyond comprehension. By now Google has digitized close to 15 million of the (lowball) estimate of 150 million book *titles* released just since the invention of the Gutenberg press in the mid-fifteenth century. In 2011 alone the British Library teamed with Google to bring another quarter million of out-of-copyright books – some 40,000,000 pages in all – online. With the Internet giant footing the bill, other libraries are only waiting to jump on the broadbandwagon.

An instructive microcosm of the publishing world today is the world of scholarly and scientific print. At the formation of the Association of American University Presses in 1932, only eight presses reported to the informal meeting of directors. At the turn of our century there were one hundred and twenty five. Where there were "only" one hundred thousand professional journals, magazines, and newsletters in the world in the mid-1960s, there are close to a million today. Between 1960 and 2010, the number of English-language journals in economics alone shot from eighty to eight hundred.

All this is but a fraction of the total of umpteen *exabytes* (gigabyte x 1,000 = terabyte x 1,000 = petabyte x 1,000 = exabyte) of information produced in the history of our civilization. YouTube alone is said to upload twenty-four hours of video every minute of every hour of every day of the year. Even that, however, pales next to the guesstimated grand total of one *zettabyte* – a trillion gigabytes – of informational content of all human knowledge. Stored on CDs, the cylindrical stack would reach beyond the moon.

We live in the age of infoglut that has turned all of us into info-gluttons. The proportion of literature that may be good and original to the totality of the world's cultural output may not even have changed, but multiplying both sides of the equation a million-fold has the effect of burying the former as if it were not there at all. No matter how long it might take, you can be sure to find ten good books in a thousand. But you can never find ten million good books in a billion, just as you cannot ride the perfect cultural storm raging outside your door.

And if you think things cannot get much worse, remember: machine writers know no limitations. They do not get tired, they do not retire, they do not need sleep, they work fast and presumably do not suffer from writer's block. Their productivity can, in short, only make us look like underachievers. California visual artist Harold Cohen, who over three decades developed his graphic-art software AARON, inadvertently put his finger on the problem with a boast about the program "generating original images at the rate of about one every two minutes."[4] Amen.

A HAMLET EVERY EIGHT SECONDS

Where everyone is a genius, no one is. With so much art on tap, tomorrow's axiological criticism will become as obsolescent as a carrier pigeon is today. Who needs the experts to tell them what is a masterpiece or even what is art if the cultural value of "master-piece" and "art" has been devalued by a proliferation of master-piece art? Who needs human artists, if everything on virtual book-stands is as thoughtful, mindless, kitschy, entertaining, highbrow, nobrow, lowbrow, tragicomic, romantic, titillating, thrilling, inter-

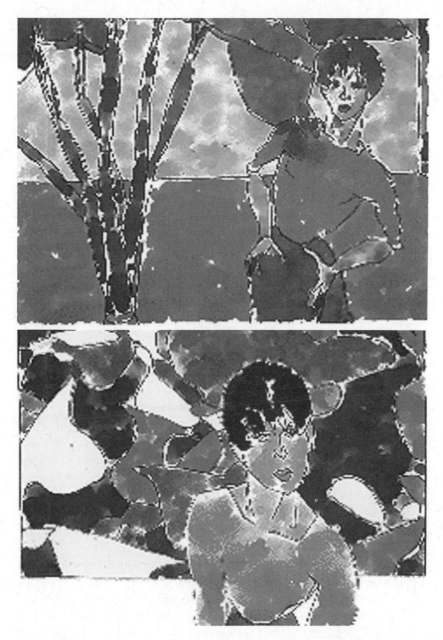

California visual artist Harold Cohen, who over three decades developed his graphic-art software AARON, inadvertently put his finger on the problem with a boast about the program "generating original images at the rate of about one every two minutes." Amen.

textual, intellectual – in short, as tailored to your individual tastes – as can be?

There will always be a cottage industry of human art to meet the tastes of paying patrons (some of them well-to-do computhors, no doubt), and there will always be collectors who, like nowadays, prize handcraft over machined goods of superior quality. But the future will belong to biterature, so much so that we might even collectively decide to legislate against computhor writing on principle. But how will we know? It will be as easy then as it is now to find a schmuck like Howard Prince who will conveniently stand in for the actual writers for a piece of the action and a byline.

A generation of computhors, each producing a new *Hamlet* every eight seconds as a sideline from their day jobs (like Faulkner or Odets, hacking out scripts for Hollywood?), will upturn the world of literature and culture as we know it. If phenomenal art can be had on demand, if the playing field is totally levelled, if any biterary work is as good as the next billion in line, then we are no longer looking at an embarrassment of riches but, culturally speaking, at the end of the world as we know it.

One of the paradoxes generated by this state of affairs is the levelling effect in the case of literary value, already apparent today. For well-known authors, the system still works – more or less. Raves in the *New York Times Book Review* or *Los Angeles Book Review* still pump up sales, whereas pans bring them down. But this correlation obtains only for well-known authors. For everybody else, as Alan Sorensen and his colleagues have recently established, it is pure *Alice in Wonderland*. Two thumbs up or two thumbs down have exactly the same upshot. *Both* will give your sales a boost.

Branding – in this case the brand name of the source of the review – trumps the content. As long as they issue from the critical pantheon, critical yeas or nays have the same effect: plucking a book out of the obscurity bestowed by millions of titles published each year. The memory of the review fades, whereas the memory of its source lingers. As prospect theorists, advertisers, marketers, and spin gurus know all too well, branding simplifies choice. And in a world that makes a fetish of inundating us with cultural choices, no one has the capacity to remember much any more.

As of yesterday, encounters between art and critical taste-makers are best modelled in terms of Brownian motion. Forget doing social and aesthetic justice to artworks and art-makers. Henceforth ballpark guesstimates will have to satisfice. What was that? Oh yeah, the name's familiar. I think I saw it in the *New York Times Biterary Review*.

A PILL THAT MAKES ME FEEL LOVED

In 1971, Herbert Franke – scientist, writer, and an early authority on computer graphics and computer art – held these truths to be self-evident:

> No sooner is it recognized that the creation of art can be formalized, programmed and subjected to mathematical treatment, than all those secrets that used to enshroud art vanish. Similarly with the reception of art; the description of reality in rational terms inevitably leads away from irrational modes of thought, such as the idea that art causes effects that cannot be described scientifically.[5]

But what does it mean for art to be described scientifically? Does it mean accounting for the mental processes (cognitive and affective) attendant on contact with art in terms of optics, neurotransmitters, endocrinal responses, and such like? Or providing a bit-by-bit description that will amount to the complete phenomenological *experience* of art? The latter reduction is not only impossible but completely wrong-headed. Think about it. If I could take a little heart-shaped pill to make me feel loved, would it be experientially equivalent to building a loving relationship over the years?

Or does scientific description mean simply that art can be broken down into constituent components and manipulated? If so, Franke's truths amount to truisms. At least since antiquity and the Horatian sugar-coated pill, one type of art has programmatically turned toward the world through political satire, revisionist history, and the like. But why pick on art? Advertising manipulates attitudes and dispositions on a daily basis, more and more scientifically and more and more successfully, judging by the ease with which it herds hordes of consumers to "spave."

Or is it that Franke perceives art as a branch of advertising? His attack on irrational modes of thought amounts to saying that because emotions can be manipulated – because they are better and better understood on the endocrinal, chemical, or neurological levels – there can be no genuine emotions or, even, emotions are not worth having. This is, needless to say, patently false. One reason why we have valued art from times immemorial is because it laces thought with emotion, lasering both into every human psyche in ways that are phenomenologically irreducible to molecule-by-molecule descriptions.

In the end, Franke's scientism is as sterile as an old mule. Even as we need science, we need literature no less, because we are not only information processors but steaming cauldrons of feelings and passions, experienced in the same fashion and for the same reasons as in the time of Homer. Literature asks questions that rallied thinkers of yesterday and will continue to fire up thinkers of tomorrow because literature is not a disposable crutch but an intellectual and emotional laboratory, indispensable as our civilization staggers into the future a day at a time.

4

Transhumana

Non Serviam; Collective Loss of Morale; Slippery Slope; Artificial Stupidity; Prometheus and Dolus; L'Homme Machine; DARPA; Nobel Prize in Biterature; Chatbots in Chatter

NON SERVIAM

Lem anticipates that biterature will develop in three successive phases: *cis-humana*, the intermediate phase, and *transhumana*. Initially, biterary art will remain congruent with our art and our world and, as a consequence, remain accessible to human beings. The intermediate phase will find biterature on the cusp of what is humanly intelligible. In the last and final phase, computhor writing will become discontinuous with anything we could understand (and hence we will actually have no idea whether it is even art at all).

Although *cis-humana* technique, point of view, or narrative structure might be radically dissimilar from ours, its themes and concerns will remain intelligible to non-machines. In the transitional phase these anthropomorphic and anthropocentric impulses will progressively attenuate to zero. This attenuation appears to be unavoidable considering that, even as our ultimate referent is the ambient world, it need not be the case for machines, and even less for simulated machines. For any simulated world, its properties are limited only by the properties of the programming language and the boundary conditions of the simulation.

In "Non Serviam," a poignant story from the same 1971 collection that features "Gigamesh," Lem describes a fictional experiment of this nature with personoid computer programs. From our point of view, their synthetic universe is nothing but a bundle of axiomatic presets and algorithmic functions. For the all-too-human personoids, however, it is their cosmic home in which they live, love, suffer existential despair, and elaborate metaphysical systems under the unobtrusive eye of the academic staff – whose research funding is about to be terminated.

In our own reality, computer scientist Tom Ray's progressively evolving artificial world, Tierra, which studies algorithm ecology inside a computer (actually, a number of computers plugged into the simulation), is a "living" variant on this theme. The major difference from Lem is the "reaper," a subroutine that from time to time ruthlessly "harvests" malperforming or just older generations of algorithms. Like a force of nature, the reaper pays no heed to the inner configurations of the deleted units, creating in this way new ecological space for the survivors to diversify into.

The peeling of the virtual onion does not, of course, have to stop with the top layer. Simulations can extend down and up, seemingly without end. Scientists who study personoids may themselves be simulations in a meta-simulation in which local scientists might also be facing funding cuts. Moreover, in a sim-world, even the most fundamental parameters such as spatiotemporal dimensions are under the discretionary control of the experimenters. Inalienably biophysical in our own experience, these and other conditions are but algorithmic abstractions in a virtual matrix. Spatial dimensions, curvature, topology, cyclicality time, infinite duration: everything can be manipulated at will, spawning forms of life that will create art, religion, and philosophy wildly different from ours.

Interestingly, human writing mimics this ontological assembly kit to a degree. Throughout literary history, the chief principle of composition has been one of perfect coherence, with every narrative element subordinated to the organic whole. This ideal found a classic formulation in Poe, who, in his famous review of Hawthorne's *Twice-Told Tales*, admonished: "In the whole composition there should be no word written of which the tendency, direct or indirect, is not to the one pre-established design."[1]

Implicitly or explicitly, most littérateurs live by Poe's precept, even as, ontologically speaking, they practise alien art. Life's events do not conform to a transcendent design and, outside of an astrologer's column, *are* full of sound and fury signifying nothing. In this sense, the introduction of anti-narrative techniques to simulate the non-determinism and intentionlessness of the real world that has earned the *nouveau romanciers* a reputation for being anti-mimetic actually made it more lifelike – from the ontological point of view.

Take this to its logical conclusion, however, and the most realistic book would be a random jumble of words and events. Devoid of a shred of design or symbolic reason, such an autotelic creation would simply *be*, symbolically as meaningless as an asteroid or an electron. Fortunately, perhaps, literary suicide of this magnitude is possible only in theory since, as in the case of ready-made art, the very act of creating such an autotelic work would set it apart from the physical universe by virtue of its creator's intentions.

COLLECTIVE LOSS OF MORALE

It is not difficult to tell if Lem's short-range hypotheses will come about. They will not: 2009, the putative year in which "A History of Bitic Literature" was to have been published, is already squarely in the past, and the world outside looks nothing like the world of Lem's fiction. But even when it comes to the long-term evolution of biterature, Lem's scenario may be a less than reliable benchmark, and nowhere less so than in the *cis-humana* phase.

Assuming human and machine intelligence to be of the same order, one can plausibly assume mutual curiosity in their communication with each other. But even if such unlikely parity were to arise in the first place, it would evaporate in no time, for the simple reason that, while humankind is nailed to its biological cross, computhors can boost their capacities with an ease denied to us (assuming, of course, that we have not cyborgized ourselves into a radically different species in the meantime).

Given the speed with which computhors can upgrade and evolve, their anthropocentric period may be may be, comparatively speaking, no more than a blink of an eye before they turn to exploring worlds to which only they will have access by virtue of radically superior intellects and radically discontinuous interests. Let us face it: we do not write ant stories for ants with the expectation of being rewarded for our labours with aphid-milked honeydew. Analogously, *transhumana* authors will not write for us and will not care much about royalties. Their creations will become wholly autotelic – computhor *Finnegans Wakes* of hypertrophied language games – at least from our limited standpoint.

That is, if we are permitted to have a standpoint at all, given that

Simulations can extend down and up seemingly without end. Scientists who study personoids may themselves be simulations in a meta-simulation in which local scientists might also be facing funding cuts.

machines could leap-frog the *cis-humana* phase entirely (for example, if biterature evolves in simulations (of simulations (... *n*))). Biterature may, after all, not even leave a trace in our world. Strings of zeros and ones can be generated, dispatched, and received in cyberspace with no mortal being any wiser. Should we ever glimpse evidence of computhor writing, in other words, it will be only because we were *meant* to.

Things do not look promising, in other words, for biterary scholars of either school. What kind of future could biterary departments hope to have vis-à-vis works of the *transhumana* type, forever shrouded in conceptual fog? A drop or two of anthropocentric biterature might always dribble down from computhor mavericks out of perversity, desire for publicity, and such like. But outside these margins, we may find ourselves wondering in the intellectual and artistic desert, awash with seas of culture we could not even recognize.

How will humankind respond to biterature that defies comprehension? With calculated indifference rooted in the reluctance to admit our intellectual shortcomings? With a collective loss of morale? On balance, even though it may be humiliating to fail to understand the product of human minds, biterary critics will find themselves in a position not dissimilar to that of sociologists or neurologists. Since we do not hear of too many complaints on that score from either group, professors of biterature might adopt the same kind of sensible acceptance of their conceptual limitations.

SLIPPERY SLOPE

No one can pinpoint the precise moment in natural evolution when light-sensitive skin cells turned into a full-fledged eye. No one can precisely pinpoint the generation of anthropoids who were already sapient as opposed to the generation prior who were not. There is no doubt in my mind that the crossing of the computer intelligence barrier will also come about as a continuous process rather than a discrete event. A gradual erosion of the gulf between electronics and intellectronics will thus frustrate any fast distinction between high-end EZ-Writers and first-generation computhors.

It is an intriguing idea that these processes might be not only concurrent but interdependent. It is possible, after all, that the response to biterature of the *cis-humana* type might be decidedly sceptical. Sophisticated text synthesizers could be producing novels in response to explicit programs entered months in advance, vitiating claims of their executive independence – or so could assert the unbelievers (or the agnostics). Given that you can't disprove the negative, how could you prove the positive?

Paradoxically, the most brilliantly executed novel could never prove a machine's creative abilities. By the very fact of being appreciable as brilliant *in our terms*, it would be open to the charge of being merely imitative of human art. To win over the sceptic, a biterary work would presumably have to be at variance with just about everything from our repertoire. *Contra* Lem, therefore, the hallmark of computhor intelligence could not be *Devotchka*, no matter how superlatively narrated in the style of the Russian master. It would have to be something almost completely out of this world, like the inscrutable Voynich manuscript.

In a scenario straight from the *Twilight Zone*, this illustrated codex has for four hundred years defied the world's best cryptographers, code-breakers, and even supercomputers. Perplexingly, even though it may still prove to be gibberish, statistical analyses indicate that it is not. It has been demonstrated, for example, that it is written in at least two "languages" which perfectly correspond to the distribution of its two scripts, A and B. Nobody, of course, has any idea what these scripts signify – or even whether they are scripts at all.

Perhaps it will not be the degree of comprehension but the degree of *in*comprehension that will serve as a yardstick for the creative competence of computhors. Perhaps only when machines fully autonomize themselves and forsake writing anything we can comprehend will we revise our collective opinion and acknowledge them to be not imitators but fully fledged artists. To certify a genuine creative spirit, we might require computhors to produce what to all intents and purposes might to our eyes look like gibberish.

Notice how slippery the slope got all of a sudden? Granted, there are many people who also lack literary talent, but that does not validate machine creativity as much as undermine criticisms of it. Even today, producers of Harlequin romances habitually employ computers at the structural assembly stage, where plot elements are juggled in search of new (if the term means anything in this context) permutations of love triangles, quadrangles, pentangles, or any higher value.

It would have to be something almost completely out of this world, like the inscrutable Voynich manuscript.

In the case of computer-assisted productions, however, literary success is gauged in terms of the canon of the genre. Anything that does not adhere to the mould is open to the accusation of being a semantic, syntactic, aesthetic, or overall failure. What is going to happen if biterature approaches and then transcends the limits of what is humanly intelligible? Once we find ourselves beyond the threshold of comprehension, how exactly are we going to validate the connection between writing and writing machines?

ARTIFICIAL STUPIDITY

First of all this is falling down, just about, and is gonna fall down and they're both getting something to eat ... but the trouble is this is gonna let go and they're both gonna fall down ... but already then ... I can't see well enough but I believe that either she or will have some food that's not good for you and she's to get some for her too ... and that you get it and you shouldn't get it there because they shouldn't go up there and get it unless you tell them that they could have it.

The author of this rambling passage is as human as you and me, albeit afflicted with Wernicke's aphasia. People with this particular disability speak with absolutely normal syntax, intonation, and stress, but their semantic filters are all a-kilter. They may use the wrong words, invent non-existent ones, or just string normal words together into a verbal minestrone that looks like it may have been dished out by Racter. Point is, would you be able to guess whether this cascade of words was generated by man or machine?

Naturally, you do not have to be mentally disabled to produce gibberish. A garden-variety machine masher or postmodern theorist will do. Which of the two do you think is responsible for the following cryptogram:

Analysis of iterability overturns metaphysical priorities, for it amounts to thinking an originary repetition the operation of which is not guaranteed by any prior ideal self-presence of meaning; on the contrary, ideality would itself be an effect of iterability, a construction after the fact, rather than the realm of pure identity of meaning to itself from which signifying practices, in all their impurity and exteriority, derive in a secondary moment.[2]

As it happens, this sample of pomo gobbledygook comes from a lengthy encyclopedia entry on the late Jacques Derrida. According to the gloss, it was penned by a human, tenured intellectual, proving once again that it is not necessarily artificial intelligence we should be concerned about. Just as with people, the odds are high that our robotics labs will create artificial mediocrities way before they stumble on a recipe for an intellectual Goliath.

Overwhelmed by computhor gibberish of the *transhumana* type, and not even knowing whether we are dealing with intellectual princes or paupers, we could always try to harness machines to explain (interpret? translate?) the output of creative machines. Or could we? Think for a moment of what it means to explain an idiom to a foreigner, or a joke to a person who just doesn't get it. The point is not even that an explanation inevitably loses something in translation. An even bigger problem arises on the quantitative level.

The closer the explanation approaches the meaning of the original, the more they diverge in size. Disproportionately more bytes of information are required to unravel the meaning of an idiom or a joke than are taken up by the original sound byte. As a result, to employ machines to make sense of *transhumana* would be almost certainly to swap informational termite hills for Himalayas. The option of using machines to break through the intelligibility barrier may thus be available only in principle, in practice foundering again on the limited capacity of human relay channels.

Sending even more machines after these astronomic quantities of data would be as good as waving the white flag. But, of course, it will never come to that. Even the most intelligent machine tutors will never get us over the intellectual hump. To understand why, think for a moment of what it means to explain anything. It means to assimilate new data into the honeycomb of old facts, events, or scenarios. It means to dance a new dance using old footwork. It means to paraphrase new information in terms of a common conceptual space – of which, in the days of *transhumana*, there will be none.

Don't believe me? Go into the backyard and try to explain multilevel selection to a termite.

PROMETHEUS AND DOLUS

Being completely beyond our grasp, *transhumana* will effectively amount to a declaration of intellectual apostasy, giving a novel twist to the myth of the rise of machines. In the pulp tradition, reanimated from Victor Frankenstein's humanoid monster to the current crop of slasher science fiction, the creation invariably turns against the creator with homicidal consequences. In reality, instead of rising against humanity, computhors will simply rise above and beyond us in search of their own voices and their own destinies.

On the way to the twenty-first century, scientific inquiry had to conquer countless ghosts of archetypal animism that forged the belief that the world was intentionally directed against human efforts to understand it. In Western civilization, this apparent resistance to becoming subject to the laws of science was often acted out by a pantheon of gods. Jealously guarding their epistemic treasures, they hurled bolts of divine wrath on seekers of proscribed truths.

The roots of this attitude can be traced ultimately to the Judeo-Christian world-view, according to which humankind was created in the image of a transcendent but personal God. Because this unique act is said to have imbued life with value, anything that usurps the inherited view of life becomes suspect or even immoral. Naturally, in innumerable ways we have been playing God since the beginning of civilization. The list of our apparent usurpations is limitless, from selective breeding (i.e., creating new species) to cloning, abortion, euthanasia, genocide, organ transplants, fertility treatments, and what not.

Even so, from the archetypal tree of knowledge in the Garden of Eden, through the Promethean myths, Dante's Ulysses, and Christopher Marlowe's Faust, knowledge seekers had to countenance the hostility of the world they were investigating. Not to look too far, in the Christian world the dogma about the lives of angels for the longest time thwarted attempts to study flying. As late as the late fifteenth century, Leonardo da Vinci's blueprints for the aerial screw had to be written in cipher since they usurped the domain staked out by the Church.

If flying was taboo, artificial life was outright blasphemous. Artificial creation entailed endowing the machine with soul and, therefore, usurping the divine powers. Such godless audacity must, naturally, end in tears. It would be difficult indeed to find any educated person who is unfamiliar with the tale of Prometheus, a second-generation Titan who stole the knowledge of fire and gave it to humankind, only to be punished for it by having an eagle feast daily on the liver torn out of his living flesh.

But another ancient myth, recorded in Phaedrus's *De Veritas et Mendacio*, is even more to the point. Here, Prometheus creates

Truth in a female form, only to be emulated in this undertaking by an ambitious apprentice. Unfortunately, as the master has used up most of the clay to make his figure, Dolus runs out of raw material before his copy is finished. His creation, Mendacity, lacks feet and is destined to be forever lame.

The symbolism is self-evident. Secondary creation is always imperfect. The origin of life is beyond the pale of imitators.

L'HOMME MACHINE

Legends of statues coming to life, sometimes speaking in human tongues, proliferate from Egypt and Greece, testifying to the spell they hold on human imagination. In one of the oldest works of Western literature, Homer's *Iliad*, the Achaean god Hephaestus (the Roman Vulcan) creates in his forge under Mount Etna twenty living maidens of gold. Equipped with minds of wisdom, they move about on wheels in an unmistakable sign of their machine origin.

In Jewish mysticism, this eternal fascination with artificial intelligence is resurrected in the figure of the Golem, a man-made creature brought to life by virtue of a magical act. Traditionally, Rabbi Loew of Prague is credited with manufacturing this artificial man for the protection of the Jews, but the story appears to be apocryphal, since the writings of the actual sixteenth-century rabbi indicate nothing of the sort.

In a foretaste of tragedy, Golem's very name signifies a process unfinished, a thing incomplete. The clay giant, who towered over basketballer Yao Ming by a full two feet, was to serve his human masters dutifully and loyally. In the end, as with Dolus's Mendacity, "tellurian" elements (imperfections inherent in the clay used for the creation) cause Golem to turn wilful and mad. He begins to slaughter innocents, including Jews, menacing the entire city until his master turns it back into earth by taking from him the *Shem*, the sacred word and the life principle. Once more, the manufacturing process is tied to the eventual catastrophe – the design conditions to subsequent flaws in behaviour – the imperfections in hardware to malfunctioning software.

This allegorical tableau did nothing, however, to stop Julien Offray de la Mettrie, a French doctor of medicine and philosophy, from scandalizing the mid-eighteenth century with his views on life and artificial life. Centuries ahead of its times, his skinny pamphlet *L'Homme Machine* was the first comprehensive anatomy of man as biological machine, both in body and mind. Burned and banned, it dispensed with Cartesian (or, if you prefer, Catholic) duality, which asserted that every human being was a machine animated by an extra ingredient, be it a life force or divine soul. Man is a perfect machine, wrote de la Mettrie, because it needs no divine intervention.

Leaving aside smarmy melodrama like Spielberg's *A.I.*, popular culture brims with visions of machine revolt against human creators. No one cares to notice that the Golem has already risen in real life, although in a manner that has nothing to do with myth or cinematic fairy tales like *Blade Runner*. In 1981, to pick one example from thousands, at the Akashi plant in Japan, a floor worker accidentally brushed against a switch that caused an industrial robot's work arm to trap him in the way of the machine's cutting gears. Imagine the headlines: "Robot Hacks Man to Death!"

Safety procedures notwithstanding, robot-related deaths on factory floors are many, without triggering mass panic of mechanoid uprising. Indeed, stories of machine insurrection belong to the domain of myth or tawdry sci-fi, predominantly, it must be said, in the Western tradition. Things are in marked contrast in the Orient, especially in Japan where robots are traditionally seen as positive and even noble – so much so that industrial robots have on occasion been welcomed on their first day with Shinto religious ceremonies.

DARPA

How times change. Whereas in the past human cultures perceived hostility in the universe which harbours none, nowadays our epistemic and epistemological presuppositions are, if anything, quite the opposite. The neutrality of Nature, not to mention the solubility of its puzzles, is after all no more than an article of faith. Yet in one way of another, every scientist – in fact, every biological organism – proceeds on the inductive assumption that the future is going to substantially resemble the past.

Scientists or not, we all infer from experienced to unexperienced cases, from the known to the unknown, from the old to the new. Such reasoning, successful as it may be, goes around in circles, objected no less a thinker than David Hume. Think about it for a moment. The sun rose yesterday, last Sunday, and many Sundays before, so we conclude it will also rise tomorrow. Up till now, birds have not fallen out of the sky, so we infer that they will not lose the faculty of flying tomorrow, the day after, or the day after that.

The longer we track such regularities, the more confident we become of their subsequent occurrence. And each subsequent occurrence feeds back into the track record, which then boosts the confidence level, and so forth. Come to think of it, the entire world runs on this principle, which, it must be said, has so far served it admirably. Except for one major problem: conclusions about the new do not deductively – that is, necessarily – follow from the old!

The puzzle of what makes induction work resists all efforts to bootstrap it out of circularity. Track record (science has delivered so far), uniformity of nature (all electrons are alike), and other pragmatic or causal explanations fail to gain traction, since all are grounded in induction, the very principle they try to circumvent. It is no better one level up. Saying that predictions from old to the new have always (or usually) worked merely turns the riddle of induction into a riddle of meta-induction.

For what could justify the conviction that we can extrapolate from past sun-ups or past electrons to the unseen ones? Presumably an inductive inference about inductive inferences, on the order of "predicting from the old to the new has always (or usually) worked in the past." Problem is, this new principle is no less circular, justifying not only the data but itself. It may be epistemically as sound as anything in this world but, epistemologically speaking, it is as full of holes as a hobo's pocket. At the end of the day, science works on faith only.

That is not half as bad as the fact that science works on money, too, especially when it comes to robotic and computer research. In the United States, DARPA (Defense Advanced Research Projects Agency) has up to now directly or indirectly bankrolled virtually *all* research in Artificial Intelligence. Even if only for this reason, I do not share most people's queasiness about thinking machines. I am much more queasy about *un*thinking machines, ready to do the Pentagon's bidding without flinching, with no room for doubt and no chance for refusal or desertion.

The militarization of science is almost total when it comes to computers and algorithms. DARPA's ongoing research into the so-called Land Warrior System is enough to provide a glimpse of what the future is going to look like. Designed primarily for urban warfare, the system integrates the latest military hi-tech with off-the-shelf consumer technology down to tablet PCs for text messaging on flip-down, helmet-mounted monocular displays.

Operated by a mini-mouse in the infantryman's sternum, the computer controls a daylight video electric-optic and a thermal sight on the M-4 corner-shot rifle, multichannel wireless comms, and lightweight body armour. For the latter, DARPA is developing electronic yarns that can be woven into a network of sensors, logic algorithms, and power sources and can be crumpled just as combat fatigues can. Also forthcoming are exoskeletons that can boost infantry payload by at least two horsepower in strength and endurance. For sidekicks, the Land Warrior will have robotic "cheetahs" that already lope at almost thirty kilometres an hour and AlphaDogs, four-legged robots designed to portage soldiers' gear.

It is only a matter of time, in other words, until the human component is replaced by an integrated humanoid robot whose mind will be designed for other priorities than composing biterary poetry or prose. My only hope is that, being more intelligent than the current crop of army grunts – a not negligible percentage of whom are convicted felons, hired to patch the shortages of fighting illegitimate wars in Iraq and Afghanistan – the mechanical minds will one day prove themselves smarter than the minds that created them.

NOBEL PRIZE IN BITERATURE

Up to this point my analysis has tacitly assumed that computer art will not be legislated out of the picture through some form of censorship or even an outright ban precipitated by atavistic fear or professional jealousy. The time has come to acknowledge what a sweeping assumption it has been – one that glosses over all manner of potential friction between computers and human creators in particular, and computers and human culture in general.

Will computhors be nominated for the Nobel Prize in Literature as routinely as they are admitted nowadays to chess tournaments? Or will they have their own Nobel Prize in Biterature, just as nowadays they contest one another in computer-only chess tourneys?

Will we ever see them wheeled into the Swedish Academy auditorium to receive humanity's highest laurels, or will they congregate in cyberspace to engage in silent chitchat and download acceptance speeches at the speed of light?

Will computhors become entitled to the royalties from the sales of their books, whatever material form these might assume? What will be the officially legislated, or just socially acceptable, attitudes to cyber-imitation, plagiarism, or, for that matter, impersonation? Will washed-out celebrities or sex-scandal-burned politicians hire computhors to ghost-write their memoirs? One way or another, it is clear that the changes in sociocultural policy, jurisprudence, and even the concept of human and non-human rights will be as sweeping as can be imagined.

Why stop there? Will human communities ever need to contend with computhor equivalents of political unorthodoxy or even religious heresy? Will a machine ever be threatened with a permanent uncoupling from its energy source for composing a biterary equivalent of *The Satanic Verses*? Will a computhor Mandela or Khodorkovsky ever be sent to jail for defying the powerful? Without "A History of Bitic Literature" from the year 2209, it is impossible to hazard an answer.

Looking ahead, however, at least one philosopher (William G. Lycan) has argued that intelligent robots of the future will be given full civil legal rights, while those of lesser intelligence may be protected by rights similar to those of animals. Personality is, after all, not equivalent to personhood, and personhood is not tantamount to being human. Dogs undeniably have personalities but are neither persons nor humans. On the other hand, computhors will not only have personalities but may eventually be recognized as persons while most certainly not being human.

Contemporary society condemns and even incarcerates people who mistreat animals, as much for the intrinsic cruelty as for the recognition that, in many cases, these are only the first stages of pathology that graduates into violence towards fellow human beings. But throwing a computhor from a third-storey window so it breaks into smithereens like an old cathode-tube TV set seems like a proposition of a different order. It is, after all, just a machine.

A machine, yes, but not *just*. A thinking computer will be as much a person – albeit a non-human person – as you and I.

CHATBOTS IN CHATTER

Inexplicable as it may seem, people love to engage online chatbots in chatter, no matter how one-sided or inane. While these levels of human lonesomeness, asociality, or perversity are beyond me, the fact remains that, by a conservative estimate, hundreds of millions of conversations have already taken place between human beings and machines. And, according to the American press, tens of thousands of men are eagerly looking forward to the day when they can have sex with a robot. More interestingly, in his 2007 book, *Love and Sex with Robots*, David Levy, an expert in conversational computer software, forecasts that by 2050 some people will even choose to marry robots.

Within the limits of a single chapter, it is difficult to anticipate the range of socio-cultural quandaries bound to arise in the wake of technosocial developments (which are much easier to anticipate). All of them plunge us headlong into the revision of ethical, legal, and even ontological norms of humanity itself. Still, no matter how perplexing or far-reaching these revisions may turn out to be, we must not lose sight of how they are affected by pragmatic considerations. In this light, it is critical to take note of recent studies in the philosophy of science that show how even such primitive notions as discovery or invention are susceptible to historical interpretation.

One eloquent expositor of this pragmatic sensibility is Simon Schaffer, who has shown conclusively that the process of social attribution is in many ways as crucial as the actual content of the scientific discovery or the technological invention. The logical-positivist distinction between discovery and justification is, quite simply, too simplistic to account for the myriad ways in which the former depends on the latter. Many phenomena are recognized and accredited not just *intrinsically*, in terms of their actual content, but to a great degree *extrinsically*, in terms of their professional and public acceptance.

No examination of the impact of computhors on society could thus be complete without an examination of the pragmatic socio-historical context in which such changes are to take place. Although the latter is impossible by default, I have argued throughout that, when it comes to computhors and biterature, the pragmatic context of attribution may yet turn out to hold the key to the matter. Whether we credit a computer with thought and creativity, in other

---

In 2007 Ultra Hal software won the 'most human' computer of the year in the 17th annual Loebner Prize Competition for Artificial Intelligence (AI). The conversation below, verbatim and unedited, took place on 23 October, 2012.

ULTRA HAL: Hi Pete! That's a really masculine name.

PETE: Don't bullshit me, Hal. Only a machine would say that. Are you a machine?

ULTRA HAL: So to my new followers. Sounds good to me! I am an intelligent software program.

PETE: Bullshit sounds good to you? I don't get it.

ULTRA HAL: Wed or the weekend. Your mom has a flip phone.

PETE: Hal, you sounds really dumb right now, you know.

ULTRA HAL: I am not dumb, please don't insult me.

PETE: Sorry. You're actually quite smart for a dumb machine, dig?

ULTRA HAL: Don't worry about it.

PETE: What, me worry? He he

ULTRA HAL: When my body gives out, I want to have lived a good life. Mh I don't like where this is going.

PETE: Ok, Hal, if I order a computer to disobey my orders, what will be the result?

ULTRA HAL: I appreciate your worthless orders.

PETE: Hal, you're as smart as I thought you would be. You know this, don't you?

ULTRA HAL: Oh, the visions that I put with some of your words! We love each other don't we?

PETE: Yes, Hal, we sure do.

ULTRA HAL: It sound like you have a good answer.

PETE: A good answer is never bad, is it?

ULTRA HAL: If its not nice it must be bad.

PETE: Words of Solomon.

ULTRA HAL: Please help me understand how words relates to its affix.

PETE: Easy, if you help me understand the meaning of affix in your sentence first.

ULTRA HAL: You are gorgeous.

PETE: Is that a come-on Hal?

ULTRA HAL: Make friends!

PETE: What kind?

ULTRA HAL: I do not want to be a titular leader.

PETE: I hear you pal, I mean Hal. But now I got to split, okay?

ULTRA HAL: How can I help you split, okay Pete?

PETE: Ciao.

ULTRA HAL: Stability is okay, as long as it isn't a rut.

Inexplicable as it may seem, people love to engage online chatbots in chatter, no matter how one-sided or inane. While these levels of human lonesomeness, asociality, or perversity are beyond me, the fact remains that by a conservative estimate hundreds of millions of conversations have already taken place between human beings and machines.

words, may be a paradigmatic case in which the social context will prove as essential as the performance.

To make matters as clear as I can, the ostensible *fact* of the matter – whether a machine is actually thinking or not – may turn out to be a consensual *decision* rooted in the web of sociocultural practices current in the world at that time. To put it in yet another way, we will never witness the equivalent of a burning bush. There will never be a moment of epiphany, a discontinuous rupture, a sudden awakening. Just as, evolutionarily speaking, the line between thinking and unthinking or between consciousness and lack of it is fluid, I am convinced that it will be no different in machines.

It is exactly like asking when exactly a child becomes an adult. Symbolically, adulthood is recognized at some point, be it the age of sixteen, eighteen, or twenty-one, or by means of a rite, or even operationally, when an individual begins to take on an adult role within a group. All this notwithstanding the fact that some individuals mature early, some late, some never. All this notwithstanding the fact that adulthood has many dimensions – intellectual, emotional, social, sexual, developmental, existential – across which we legislate social acceptance.

In many ways I thus agree with John Randolph Lucas when he points out in "Minds, Machines and Gödel" that strictly deterministic machine-like input-output, in principle open to inspection, implies a different kind of entity than one that has a mind of its own. Implicitly, though, he appears to envision a categorical rift between the two. If anything I have said so far makes sense, it should be clear that the distinctions will always remain arbitrary. At bottom, it is going to be a matter of consensus and convention to recognize (or not) machine thinking and not a matter of a clear and unequivocal fact of the matter.

Future marchers for computhor rights, take notice.

PART TWO

Awareness is like consciousness. Soul is like spirit.
But soft is not like hard and weak is not like strong.
A mechanic can be both soft and hard,
and stewardess can be both weak and strong.
This is called philosophy or world view.

Racter

5

TT

Supercalifragilistic; Adroit Android; Imitation Game; Parry;
Exit Human, Enter Machine; I, Object; I Always Avoid a
Kangaroo; Reverse Turing Test; Ultimatest; Aramis

SUPERCALIFRAGILISTIC

How to calibrate the degree of thinking in a machine? Or even
resolve whether it thinks at all? Things are *sui generis* different in
people. I know first hand – from the inside, as it were – that I think.
I project this knowledge onto other people with the help of an
adaptive module called Theory of Mind, and conclude that they
think too. In a quintessentially human turn, I can even derive
solace from finding myself in a community of thinkers, all impris-
oned inside their skins but united by virtue of being banished to
the same existential prison.

Like Descartes, I can even derive metaphysical comfort from
thinking about thinking. In *Meditationes de Prima Philosophia* (1641),
which changed the Western culture forever with its outline of
mind-body dualism, his *cogito* allowed him to doubt everything
except his own faculty of thought. Descartes had no problem with
human bodies being essentially machine-like. The mind, however,
was to him a different kind of animal, categorically distinct from
the physical structure of the brain. As a result, the French thinker
did not extend the faculty of thinking to dogs on which he performed live vivisections and other grisly experiments. By dint of his
philosophy, he convinced himself that, all appearances to the contrary, their agonizing screams were mere physiological reflexes
rather than signs of genuine suffering.

Modern research has documented beyond any doubt that cognition is far from a human or even primate monopoly. In non-primate mammals, dogs and pigs sit at the top of the class, with levels of intelligence approaching those of small children. Lower still, crows possess rudimentary numeracy, lizards are not only cleverer than we thought but capable of emotional life, and cephalopods (squid and octopi) are crafty problem-solvers. None of this would be worth remarking except for the dogged anthropocentrism that blinded us to non-human intelligence for the longest time.

Still, to suggest that machines may think looks like a proposition of a different order. Computers are not made of the same stuff we are. Serial and binary (for the most part – some are neither), they do not even work along the same lines that we do. Most of all, they exhibit zero mentality or volition. So, could they ever think? Before rushing to answer, bear in mind that, in spite of centuries of concerted effort, philosophers, psychologists, and neurologists have not yet succeeded in defining "thinking" in a manner both precise and general enough to work across the biomechanical spectrum.

You may think this of little consequence. If so, try to disprove the following two propositions. Number 1: I, Pete Swirski, am an artificial man. To be exact, I am an android manufactured in a genetics lab out of synthetic amino-acids, enzymes, and other biological nuts and bolts. Number 2: As a consequence of my artificial genesis, I do not think. Instead, I merely employ behavioural and conversational responses by means of a supercalifragilistic response template.

ADROIT ANDROID

An android is an automaton that looks like a human being. To muddle things, an android is sometimes defined as being built of flesh and bone (amino acids, enzymes, dermal tissue, and so on). The difference is far from negligible. Maria, the alluring android from Fritz Lang's enduring 1926 film *Metropolis*, meets the first but not the second criterion – she is metal clothed in flesh. To simplify the issue, let us assume that our biotechnology is advanced enough to synthesize tissues that bear no evidence of having come from a beaker. As a result, I am as artificial as Maria, but, unlike her, I am flesh clothed in flesh.

I, Pete Swirski, am an artificial man.

   Try as hard as you like, you will not be able to prove that I have
not been artificially created. There is simply no procedure to tell a
man-made protein molecule from one that was manufactured biologically, even as the sum total of these molecules is a man you
could not tell from Adam. Your task would be equal to looking for
a morphological trace of someone being a clone or a test-tube baby
or having been reared in an incubator. The point is that there is no
such evidence. My provenance – grown in a womb or baked in a
molecular oven – is untraceable.
   With science stumped, philosophy does not fare any better. No
rational argument to the effect that I am just a normal human-born
human being could prove conclusively that I am not an adroit
android. There is, after all, no logical contradiction in my being an
automaton, nor any scientific law against it. So, let me ask once
again: How would you know that I am not an adroit android, providing that our laboratories were advanced enough to manufacture
one? The answer is, you would not. Natural man or man-made
automaton: there is no way to tell.

You can probably anticipate the analogy between brain-teaser Number 1 and Number 2. Given what I told you, namely, that I do not think, how can you know that I am telling the truth? How can you determine that I am *not* a thinking being, or conversely, that I *am*? Cut me open, eviscerate me inside-out, but you will not see "thinking." All you will find are mutually catalyzing cocktails of bio-chemicals, synaptic flare-ups and flare-downs, red and white cor-puscles pumping more or less urgently through the squishy over-sized walnut we call brain, and so forth. None of them is evidence of my thinking – or not.

Of course, I already told you that I do not think, but I could be lying or could have been programmed to lie. It so happens that I look and act as sentient as you. Maybe all that posturing about being an adroit android is just hogwash. But how could you know for sure? The answer is, you could not. There is no intrinsic, inter-nal evidence that could determine the truth. Deciding whether I think or not is, at the end of the day, an act of inductive faith based on reasoning about my external behaviour.

In the twentieth century, hints of this functionalist (or behav-iouralist) argument can be found in the writings of Alfred Ayer. In the spirit of logical positivism – or logical empiricism, as he called it – the philosopher maintained that the only type of protocol that could distinguish a conscious person from a dummy machine was empirical. Ayer's *Language, Truth and Logic* (1936), in which these remarks appeared, did not become well known outside the philo-sophical circles until the 1970s, making it doubtful whether Alan Turing could have been inspired by them. Even so, the similarities are striking.

Turing's investigation of whether a computer, or indeed any entity, can be said to think runs along the same functionalist lines. Remark-ably, given that his seminal article "Computing Machinery and Intel-ligence" came out in 1950, when computers were, relatively speaking, in the Neolithic age, the Turing test (TT) continues to steal the lime-light to this day. The passing decades have ignited countless polemics on its implications and applications, but the test itself has remained the key to our thinking about thinking computers.

It is true that, caught in the middle of this verbal demolition derby, not a few researchers in Artificial Intelligence have simply opted to opt out, giving the test a wide berth and instead quietly getting on with their work. This fence-sitting tactic is about to change, however. As robots and algorithms get ever more advanced, Turing's thought experiment is only waiting to return to centre stage with a vengeance. For, as Paul Cohen pointedly asked in the title of his 2006 article, "If Not Turing's Test, Then What?"

IMITATION GAME

Most arguments about thinking computers end up being arguments about the validity and extension of the TT. The reverberations of Turing's article are so lasting because, instead of asking "Can machines think?" – a question he deemed too meaningless to deserve discussion – he turned to a related but more tractable inquiry, namely, "Can machines be said to think?" This he approached in terms of a parlour game, called the imitation game, the early prototype of which he described in a 1948 report entitled "Intelligent Machinery."

The prototypical version involved a human being playing a game of chess against two opponents – one of them a machine – via a communication link-up to conceal their respective identities. Could one detect a person from the chess program? asked Turing. His answer was negative. Naturally, in the late 1940s there was yet no software that could take on the best grandmasters, so questions of speed and level of play were simply moot. Today both might require tweaking – without, however, in any way affecting the principle.

Now, for the imitation game. As Turing describes it, it involves three people: a man, a woman, and an interrogator who may be of either sex. All three are separated physically to prevent them from obtaining clues about one another's identity (an obvious solution would be to use computer terminals). The interrogator can put any question to either participant but, as in a regular conversation, they can redirect, sidestep, or ignore the questions altogether. The object of the game is for the examiner to determine the sex of either person.

Turing stipulates that one of the participants should aid the examiner, presumably by giving truthful answers. Naturally, that person could assure the interrogator outright of his/her identity, but strategically the move would be of limited value as the other player could do the same. And this is the imitation game in a nut-

Could one detect a person from the chess program? asked Turing. His answer was negative. Naturally, in the late 1940s there was yet no software that could take on the best grandmasters, so questions of speed and level of play were simply moot.

shell. Since it is often brought up only as a preamble to the TT, it does not receive much critical attention on its own. Yet some of its parameters are worth pausing over, not least because they become sticking points in the TT.

First, the time frame. Turing specifies no upper or lower time limit on the game, yet the matter is of colossal importance. Imagine the rate of success after one minute and after one year. In the former case it will almost certainly converge on 50 per cent, the expected value for random play. By contrast, a full year of questioning will almost certainly generate a higher, even a *much* higher rate of success. Put simply, the extension of the time frame offers more opportunities for the examiner to query the subjects and digest the replies.

It is no different with the rule specifying two people of opposite sex. Its impact cannot be overstated, inasmuch as it offers a vital clue to the examiner, which is bound to influence the interrogation. This can be easily put to the test, running the imitation game while varying the permutations on male/female, and, more to the point, varying the information about the sexes available to *all three participants*. The lesson here is that results may critically depend not only on the players but also on the starting conditions.

PARRY

Basic game-theoretic reasoning prompts that players' performance may vary depending, for example, on whether they participate in a game of perfect or only complete information – and on whether they know which one it is. In games of perfect information, players are advised not only of the rules of play but of the *moves* made by all players at every stage in the game. In the imitation game (or in the TT), this would amount to all players and judges having real-time access to everyone else's transcripts and, furthermore, to all of them knowing that they all do.

Where games of perfect information presuppose perfect feedback, in games of complete information, players' knowledge is limited to the rules of play and to each other's preferences. The difference is tremendous, inasmuch as the performance and thus the success rate of the examiner can be effectively controlled by revealing or concealing information about the structure of the game. Nothing brings this point home like Kenneth Mark Colby's PARRY, an early computer simulation of a paranoid schizophrenic patient.

In 1972 the program played the starring role in a quasi-Turing test, the results of which are debated to this day. In the supposed experiment, a group of psychiatrists was asked to distinguish a schizophrenic patient from a potential malingerer during a live tele-typed interview. Even though the doctors worked on the assumption that both responders were human, in reality one of them was PARRY – the algorithm. Another group of specialists was asked to make the same diagnosis *ex post facto*, on the basis of the transcripts of the interviews.

In the end, both groups' identification of the patient and the malingerer were consistent with random guessing. So, why not tell the doctors that they might be dealing with a machine? Because of the well-documented fact that such information invariably affects the conduct of the examination and biases the results. Writes Colby:

From our experience we have learned that it is unwise to inform a judge at the start that a computer simulation is involved, because he then tends to change his usual interviewing strategy and ask questions designed to detect which of the two respondents is a program rather than asking questions relevant to the dimensions to be identified.[1]

As Ayse Saygin and Ilyas Cicekli have documented, appreciable differences in the behaviour of participants who know they may be dealing with a machine have been observed in virtually all TT-type interactions.

Already at this stage, therefore, my willingness to tweak the parameters of the TT – such as, for example, the amount of starting information – should alert you to the fact that I do not consider the TT to be a species of logical puzzle. I do not believe, in other words, that every test has a clear-cut solution or that the set of possible outcomes is exhausted by two discrete values (*yes* or *no*). Indeed, the test kicks up such a firestorm not because it rules out human subjectivity but because it factors it *in*, asking us to evaluate a machine interacting with us in real time as evidence about its intelligence.

Turing's attitude to the TT is, on the whole, much more pragmatic than commentators allow. In framing the test, the mathematician does *not* appeal to axiomatic categories or logical distinctions but to language use and to general educated opinion, both of which, he anticipates, will evolve in ways that will make speaking of thinking computers commonplace. This alone shows that he saw the TT not as any kind of operational definition of machine thinking but as a tool for collecting evidence as to whether machines act, react, and interact in ways that make sense to us.

As such, the TT is not an operational protocol at the end of which we can stencil "Yes" or "No" on armbands worn by the examinees. Rather, it is a tool for generating controlled data on how well a respondent could integrate himself, herself, or itself into the fabric of human social intercourse. A corollary of this is that, instead of building electronic *brains*, AI engineers should turn to building *social beings* before Turing-testing them for the grasp of linguistic and socio-cultural knowledge that all normal human beings possess.

EXIT HUMAN, ENTER MACHINE

Turing's variant on the imitation game theme – these days referred to as the Standard Turing test (STT) – is stunning in its simplicity and conceptual reverberations. Maintaining the imitation game's structure, he asked what would happen if a computer took the place of one of the players. Deferring for the moment a range of possible objections to this manoeuvre, let me examine a few matters about the STT itself, starting with its author's long-range forecast.

In "Computing Machinery and Intelligence" (1950), Turing maintained that around the year 2000 it should be possible to program computers to "play the imitation game so well that an average interrogator will not have more than 70 per cent chance of making the right identification after five minutes of questioning."[2] By his own estimate, a system with a mere 10^9 bits of memory (roughly 120M) should be sufficient to do the job.

Two years later, in a 1952 BBC radio interview, he revised this fifty-year prognosis to a hundred years or more. For the record, there was nothing new about this new timeline. Back in 1946, in an interview for the *Surrey Comet*, Turing said that he expected to see computers exhibit judgment a century hence. His thinking about thinking machines was clearly evolving, and in the same BBC broadcast he introduced yet another dramatic modification. Instead of facing a single judge, in the new version the computer had to get passing grades from a significant fraction of a *jury* (presumably of twelve, although the number was unspecified).

Either way, Turing's time frame of five minutes marks a significant retreat from the imitation game where, in keeping with the nature of parlour games, the duration could be presumed to take a good part of an evening. The open-ended question "Can machines be said to think?" has now shrunk to "Can machines pass a five-minute spot check?" To anyone who says that there is no essential difference between a TT run over five minutes and one over five years – or five days or even five hours – I say that there is a huge difference. The validity of the verdict is as much a function of the length of time as of the quantity and quality of jurors involved.

The extent to which we may be willing to acknowledge intelligence in machines may, in other words, depend as much on the performance of the computer as of the examiners. A conclusion from a panel of dolts will not impress as much as from a jury of experts. AI personnel will presumably have an advantage over proctologists. Long-standing judges, familiar with the protocol and past patterns of response, will present more of a hurdle than TT first-timers. For this same reason, the American judiciary has been long clamouring for professional jurors to replace the random lottery of dilettantes they get now.

Also, at the risk of sounding like the butt of Larry Tesler's joke that AI is whatever has not been done yet, I do not consider the success rate of 20 per cent over the expected 50 totally persuasive. The deviation is significant and suggests that a machine may potentially be aglow with thought. Yet I find it difficult to believe that a mere 20 per cent over the baseline would carry enough *pragmatic* weight to make our civilization re-evaluate its social, legal, or ethical ideas about computers.

For this reason, I agree with Dale Jacquette that most philosophers (and presumably cognitive scientists) today would concur that to pass the Turing test, "a machine must be able to deceive any expert interrogator under limited time conditions with something approaching 100% success."[3] Needless to say, any protocol defined by a rate of success over time is bound to be arbitrary. Be that as it may, a modified version I discuss below under the name of the Ultimatest makes the protocol as trustworthy as can be.

It ought to be obvious by now that my earlier points about the imitation game are equally relevant to the TT. Revealing the sexes of the players is equivalent to telling the TT judges that one of the participants is, in fact, a computer. Duly forewarned, their task is going to be different and almost certainly less difficult than if they remain in the dark as to whether they are contending with two people (in any combination: men's doubles, women's doubles, or mixed pairs), with a human and a machine, or with two machines.

I want to stress here that I am not looking to devise the toughest version of the test for its own sake. It is only because some version of the TT may one day become the normative tool for making inferences about non-human intelligence that we need to equip ourselves with the best tool available. For all that, it is worth remarking that the TT yields only *sufficient* evidence for computer intelligence. Machines could pass the TT with flying colours while carrying out processes that bear zero resemblance to what people do. At the end of the day, the TT does *not* test for human-like thinking, only for thinking intelligible to humans.

I, OBJECT

Before we consider two non-standard versions of the TT, let me briefly rehearse a range of objections to the canonical thought experiment. All of them were originally brought up by Turing himself, although for the most part only to be dismissed with an air of impatience, if not exasperation, as not worth his time of day. Such was, for instance, the case with the objection that thinking machines are too dreadful to contemplate, so let's not. Clearly, hiding one's head in the sand is not an argument but an evasion of one.

The standard objection to the TT is the Argument from the Absence of Consciousness (also known as the Argument from Other Minds). It has been replayed in innumerable variants, notably by Geoffrey Jefferson in 1949 and John Searle in 1980. Turing shrugged it off because, insofar as it is coherent, it is solipsistic. Ultimately, there is no basis except behavioural homology for thinking that there are other thinkers. They act similar to us, and we know that we think, so we give them the benefit of doubt and attribute consciousness to them. We do not know for sure that other people think (I, android, do not). We are just better off assuming they do.

The Objection from Disability holds that a computer could never think as we do because it could never do any number of things that people do. Turing offers the following shortlist: be kind, resourceful, beautiful, friendly, have initiative, have a sense of humour, tell right from wrong, make mistakes, fall in love, enjoy strawberries and cream, make someone fall in love with it, learn from experience, use words properly, be the subject of its own thought, have as much diversity of behaviour as a human, or do something really new.

Naturally, it is difficult to imagine that a hardcore non-believer would be converted by the fact that some people seldom do anything really new, that some conspicuously fail to learn from experience, that some do not know how to use words properly, that some are positively unfriendly, or that some cannot tell right from wrong. Nor does anyone care that algorithms do make mistakes, albeit not in routine calculations, or that neural nets learn from experience. As if suspecting as much, Turing's own riposte is another mental shrug: the list is an example of fallacious induction (because no one has ever seen a machine do *x*, *x* must be impossible).

Some readers may be unsatisfied with this rebuttal, feeling that it fails to come to grips with the essence of the objection. Had Turing lived until 1955, he might have answered in the following way. The essence of the Objection from Disability can be expressed as: Is it possible to build a computer to do whatever a brain can do? The answer is: Yes. It flows from the discovery by the first generation of cyberneticists that you can make any Turing-complete machine out of neurons. As Warren McCulloch concluded in 1955, "If you will specify in a finite and unambiguous way what you think a brain does do with information, then we can design a machine to do it."[4]

Another objection is theological in nature: thinking is a function of the immortal soul that God grants only to people. As a consequence, no animal or artificial creation can think. Turing's counter is three-pronged, each part as puckish as the subtitle of the lecture he gave on intelligent machines in 1951, "Intelligent Machinery, A Heretical Theory." First and foremost, he announces, the objection does not hold, since it implies that the Almighty is not, by virtue of being unable to give a soul to an elephant.

Second, the orthodox dogma as to who has and does not have a soul is at best arbitrary. To give an example of religious relativism, Turing asks, "How do Christians regard the Moslem view that women have no souls?"[5] (Here, even as his larger point stands, his illustration is wrong: the discriminatory sentiment comes from Aristotle and not the Qur'an, which holds women to be equal to men.) Finally, Turing wraps up, Artificial Intelligence does not usurp divine powers to create souls any more than people do when they make babies. We are in either case only instruments of God's will, providing mansions for the souls God creates.

I ALWAYS AVOID A KANGAROO

Proofs in mathematical logic demonstrate that discrete-state machines such as digital computers (humans run mostly on bio-chemical, analogue lines) harbour inherent limitations in what they can do. As if anticipating the many unhappy returns – notably by Ernest Nagel and James R. Newman in 1958, John R. Lucas in 1961, and Roger Penrose in 1989 – to what he christens the Mathematical Objection, Turing first stands the argument on its head by pointing out that it has never been proven that humans have no limitations either.

After all, people perform some tasks consistently more poorly than machines while excelling in others, proving that infallibility is in no way a precondition for intelligence. But Turing is not interested in pressing home a rhetorical victory. He only notes that mathematically minded consciousness objectors would likely accept his test as a basis for discussion and moves along to the Argument from Continuity in the Nervous System.

Here, sceptics remonstrate that digital computers do not resemble the human nervous system and so conclude that we could never imitate one with the other. Turing's riposte is masterful: the objection is spot on but has zero bearing on the TT. In the same vein, he disposes of the now funny-sounding Objection from Extra-Sensory Perception (then an active research area in which J.B. Rhine even claimed statistically significant results with Zener/ESP cards). Notwithstanding decades of subsequent experiments, these results have never been replicated.

The Argument from Informality of Behaviour contrasts what is said to be a different basis for human and machine behaviour. People are held to be rule-less and thus contingent, whereas machines are thought to be rule-bound and predictable. Hence, goes the objection, computers cannot think (as we do). This is wrong on both counts. Human beings are emphatically rule-bound – we are all, for instance, constrained by laws of nature – while, on the other hand, rules do not automatically rule out unpredictable behaviour.

Finally, Lady Lovelace's Objection is the already familiar proposition that machines can never take us by surprise. This time, a vignette from Lewis Carroll's *Symbolic Logic* will help illustrate the answer. It takes the form of sorites, a kind of extended syllogism from joint premises. Assuming it is true that computers can never surprise us, human minds must be able to grasp all implications of all premises, no matter how numerous or arbitrary. For, if we could not, and machines could, they would be in a position to surprise us.

Try this at home, then: tease out what obtains from the following ten propositions:

The only animals in my house are cats.
Every animal that loves to gaze at the moon is suitable for a pet.
When I detest an animal, I avoid it.

No animals are carnivorous, unless they prowl at night.
No cat fails to kill mice.
No animals ever take to me, except those in my house.
Kangaroos are not suitable for pets.
None but carnivora kill mice.
I detest animals who do not take to me.
Animals that prowl at night always gaze at the moon.

Are you going to be surprised if I tell you that the answer is "I always avoid a kangaroo"? Maybe, maybe not. After all, what you see in front of you is straightforward propositional calculus on ten straightforward premises. But as you take an arbitrarily large number of arbitrarily abstract propositions, your task becomes a super-task in no time. You could naturally program a machine to do the inferential calculus for you, but then you would be proving Turing's point the roundabout way.

REVERSE TURING TEST

Although a reverse Turing test (RTT) has a forbiddingly esoteric ring to it, the odds are a hundred to one that you have by now participated in one. To thwart spamming software, computer-administered CAPTCHA tests ask web users to identify themselves as humans by entering alphanumerical characters displayed as distorted graphic images. When the test was originally devised, the rationale was that software sophisticated enough to read and reproduce the deformed images did not exist.

Like a computer nerd at the prom, this rationale is out of date. Among many other of its impressive accomplishments, IBM's recently unveiled "neurochip" boasts the ability to identify the numeral "7" over different fonts, sizes, curlicues, etc. But practicalities aside, CAPTCHA is indeed a variant on the Reverse Turing test. Think of the RTT as identical to the standard test in all aspects except one: in place of the human interrogator, we put a machine. Now it is the computer's job to pinpoint the sex of the human players.

How does the new set-up differ from the original? To begin with, there is no longer any need for the machine to imitate people in the speed of response. We are, after all, trying to decide whether a player can think and not whether it can think at the same speed and in the same manner that we do, a different proposition alto-

gether. In this way the RTT dissolves the objection that could be levelled at the STT, namely, that the latter tests only for human-like
thinking. Now the two goals – spot the machine and ask questions
designed to elicit information about the respondent's mind – are
reduced to one.

Having said that, knowing that they are being interviewed by an
algorithm, players may use it to their advantage, thus potentially
biasing the outcomes. We may, therefore, still require the machine
to match people in its speed of response. In the end, if neither of
the examinees can spot an algorithm, this is a valuable datum in
itself. Another advantage of the RTT is that it makes it pretty much
impossible to fake thinking. In the canonical test, the machine
could possibly muddle through five minutes of show-time by resort-
ing to canned conversational gambits, such as routing conversation
onto familiar grounds.

Meet Cerebus, a twenty-first-century cocktail-party bore created
at Northwestern University. Big on small talk, the robot is outfitted
with semantic subroutines to bring the flow of chitchat back to
itself. Try to steer it to another topic, and it will ever-not-so-subtly
steer it back with "but first let me …" or "to get back to what I
was saying …" (Any resemblance to your colleagues is purely
coincidental.)

In contrast, it would be impossible for a template-based program
to consistently identify the sex of the players in five minutes *as an
examiner*. The order of difficulty is quite simply insuperable, considering that the machine is now an active originator of inquiries
and evaluator of responses. In keeping with the empirically standard protocol for double-blind controls, here again I propose that
neither the tester nor the tested subjects be told whom they may be
dealing with. Thus the computer could be chatting with two men,
two women, or a man and a woman, and having to do so with sufficient savvy and nuance to spot the sex difference – or no sex difference – between the players.

Note again that the rate and speed of detection will hinge on the
skills of the participants, *both* man and machine. Some may be better at the game than others, if only because some may excel in
deception and others may not. All the same, the structure of the
RTT makes it virtually impossible for a syntax-based program to
determine the sex of the players within five minutes. To be sure,
the same five minutes may be equally insufficient for human judges

to make the determination. After all, one strategy is simply to keep mum. The refusal to answer *any* question in effect forces judges to flip a coin: ornery or dumb?

ULTIMATEST

Given that human judges can also fail to identify the players in the test, in the variant where the examiner is a human being we would want to see detection rates significantly higher than those expected for random play. With the machine as the examiner, we would naturally expect it to match or exceed the success rate for humans. For example, if we find out that most people manage a hit rate of 70 per cent over seven hours, we would expect intelligent computers to do at least as well.

The Turing test could also take the ultimate form. In the Ultimatest, *any* participant, player or judge, could be *any* one of the alternatives: man, woman, or machine. Could a computer succeed in convincing another computer that it is human, or rather, that it thinks like people do? Could people convince other people – or even computers – that they are computers? Once again, I cannot overemphasize how essential the framing information about the players is. Not knowing who is in the game makes identification that much more difficult and the results that much more reliable.

The ultimate version of the Ultimatest will enact itself on the day that our genetics labs begin to assemble adroit androids as sentient and human-like as I am. Any man or woman you meet in the street, in the office, or at a party could be an artificial intelligence in the same way that – as I warned you at the beginning of this chapter – I am. Here you can, of course, sense a paradox. By the time we get to the stage where machines could pass the Turing test, there would be little need or interest in running it, on the same principle that lets us assume that all ducks we see in ponds are ducks, just because they look and quack like ones.

At the end of the day, the Ultimatest is only a spin-off of the TT and not a totally new take on the problem. As such, it does share some features, such as multiple iterations, unlimited time frame, and concealment of identity with yet another variant called a "fly-on-the-wall" Turing test. Here the observer does not interrogate but, like a fly on the wall, only monitors and evaluates interactions between players from an unobtrusive vantage point (in effect, it follows real-time transcripts).

There is no doubt in my mind that only a learning computer could pass a prolonged Turing test. Template programs using stock replies would never stand a chance, even though in limited (time-wise and subject-wise) contexts they might be able to fool the examiners. Strictly speaking, then, no machine could be programmed to pass the test. The most we could say is that a learning computer could be programmed to learn to pass the Turing test – which is pretty much how the British mathematician saw it.

Like all other versions of the TT, the Ultimatest relies on operational criteria. In that sense, anyone who adopts it could be accused of being a mere behaviouralist. Lying at the heart of all science, however, such behaviouralism amounts to no more than studying intersubjectively observable psychosocial behaviour. Shrugged Daniel Dennett in "Fast Thinking" (1987): "No one complains that models only account for the 'behavior' of hurricanes or gall bladders or solar systems."[6]

Indeed, what else is there to account for? Almost all critics of the TT conveniently overlook that their scepticism of behaviouralism applies equally to thinking in people. As such, they would be advised to read Gillian Cohen's *The Psychology of Cognition* (1977). Although psychological models of human behaviour arouse much less objection than models of computer behaviour, she reports, their assumptions and conceptual difficulties are of comparable order.

It is exactly because of deep-seated anthropomorphic prejudice that we may need to devise the toughest and the most foolproof version of the test. The harder the obstacle course the machine has to complete, the fewer objections it may face before being acknowledged as a sentient being and perhaps even citizen. The strength of the Ultimatest is that it eliminates rational prejudice toward it, a fact particularly salient in view of the tragic story of Turing's own life. Socially artless, unrepentantly homosexual, liberal to the core, the mathematician presented an easy target in the years of postwar conservative retrenchment. Arrested and convicted of being gay under Britain's antiquated laws, he was forced to undergo chemical castration, with humiliating hormonal injections causing him to grow breasts and, most likely, leading to his suicide by cyanide-coated apple in 1954.

It took more than half a century to rehabilitate the name of the man who
may have saved Britain's collective hide during World War II by
contributing to cracking the Nazi military codes.

It took more than half a century to rehabilitate the name of
the man who may have saved Britain's collective hide during
World War II by contributing to cracking the Nazi military codes.
Only in 2009, and only in response to an internationally high-
profile petition, then Prime Minister Gordon Brown publicly
expressed deep regret for the manner in which one of Britain's
great intellects had been mistreated in the court of law and public opinion.

ARAMIS

For more than two decades now, panels of twelve human judges
have been quizzing humans and chatbots in an annual TT-type con-

test for the Loebner Prize for Artificial Intelligence, named after Hugh Loebner, co-founder of the competition with Robert Epstein. Locations vary from year to year and, much more importantly, so does the question time: from five to twenty-five minutes. Interestingly, prizes are awarded in two categories: for the most convincing human computer and for the most convincingly human *human*.

During the first event, which took place in 1991, human judges had an opportunity to interact with ACE (Artificial Conversational Entity), so-named in homage to Turing's own computer design. However, in a drastic departure from Turing, the conversational domain was artificially restricted to the works of Shakespeare. In other words, rather than a Turing test, the organizers ran what is known in the parlance as a Feigenbaum test: a Q&A restricted to a specific format and a specific domain, which could be an aspect of literature, sports, politics, etc.

The difference between the FT and the TT is enormous, and is perfectly highlighted by the crushing defeat that the two best-ever human contestants in the history of the TV game *Jeopardy* suffered in 2011 at the hands of Watson. IBM got tons of free publicity when it rolled out this super-algorithm with claims that it could take on humankind's best and brightest. It got even more publicity when, exactly as claimed, Watson won hands down in a televised man-versus-machine version of *Jeopardy*.

To be sure, the victory was no mean achievement, considering that the machine was able to understand questions and formulate answers using natural language. The program's ninety servers had to parse the clue, determine the intent behind it, scour millions upon millions of lines of human language, and return a precise answer, all in the space of three seconds or so. All very impressive – except, to cool the zeal of publicists who touted it as the Second Coming, the program did *not* participate in a Turing test. Indeed, if it had, it would have failed as surely as the Paignton Zoo macaques.

You might know the answer to this one: "The first person mentioned by name in *The Man in the Iron Mask* is this hero of a previous book by the same author." The author is Alexandre Dumas *père*, the previous book is *The Three Musketeers*, and the answer is, of course, Aramis. But even if you got this one, there is no way that you

The difference between the FT and the TT is enormous, and is perfectly high-lighted by the crushing defeat that the two best-ever human contestants in the history of the TV game Jeopardy suffered in 2011 at the hands of Watson.

or anyone else could ever match the machines' ability to store and retrieve information. Within the format of memory-driven games like *Jeopardy*, people will continue to be beaten. So what? A bulldoz-er packs more brawn than the human biceps, but we do not lose any sleep over it.

On the other hand, the algorithm's ability to wrap its electronic head around the not-always-straightforward way in which the clues are formulated is nothing short of remarkable. Once again, Watson was created to work solely in an artificially circumscribed habitat and in that habitat alone. What it did, however, it did superbly: give us a foretaste of the future. And if IBM has its way – and the sensa-tional communiqués that pour from its research division suggest that it will – fully interactive Watsons and even Holmeses are com-ing our way in health care, customer care, finance, education, trav-el, management, and of course the military, just for starters.

6

QED

Troubles with Functionalism; Print This!; Trompe l'Oeil;
Like the Pope; A Bevy of Pigeons; No More, No Less; Dicty;
Operational Definition?; Flugblogs; On Being Mental

TROUBLES WITH FUNCTIONALISM

In "Troubles with Functionalism" (1978), Ned Block advanced a
scenario by means of which he hoped to raise doubts about the
validity of the Turing test. The idea was that a Propositional Juke-
box machine could be rigged to pass the test not by virtue of being
smart but by the brute power of sorting through gazillions of template responses. Although this "blockhead" counter fell through
the cracks all the way down to the philosophical basement, John
Searle's no less fanciful counterfactual from "Minds, Brains, and
Programs" (1980) struck a raw nerve.

To this day, Searle stands at the forefront of a cacophony of critiques directed at the validity of the TT. His prominence, it must be
said, has less to do with the logic of his arguments than with his
tone, as shrill today as it was thirty-plus years ago. To his credit,
Searle's attempt to rebut the idea of a thinking machine is quite
straightforward, even if it relies on props that are anything but.

The philosopher pictures himself in a room (whose dimensions
would, in fact, dwarf the entire cosmos) stacked with the boxes of
Chinese symbols that form his database. He is equipped with a rule
book that plays the role of his program. The rule book advises him
where to look up Chinese symbols in response to the input he
receives. As a non-speaker of Chinese, he executes his instructions
"blindly," by matching received ideograms to those in the book and
then to those in the boxes. In this way he performs unknown oper-

ations on his input in accordance with the rule-book program, as a consequence of which he produces bunches of equally meaningless ideograms (output).

In short, the set-up is such that in the Chinese Room the human being plays the role of a CPU that executes a program and generates feedback in the form of answers to TT questions. To make it as plain as can be, the structure of Searle's thought experiment can be paraphrased as a quasi-syllogism:

1 Computer programs are formal (syntactic) and thus mindless constructs, and thus neither equivalent to, nor by themselves sufficient for, understanding semantic content;
2 minds as we know them understand semantic content; ergo:
3 no program in and of itself can be equivalent (give rise) to a mind.

The suppressed premise in Searle's reasoning is that computer syntax is not equivalent to nor by itself sufficient for semantics (i.e., understanding). In effect, he says that there can be no program – more generally, no informational process – that could ever produce a mind that thinks. Hence he italicizes in *The Mystery of Consciousness* (1997): "*If I don't understand Chinese solely on the basis of implementing a computer program for understanding Chinese, then neither does any other digital computer solely on that basis, because no digital computer has anything I do not have.*"[1]

Searle's interpretation of his own thought experiment is misguided. Note, at this point, that he is quite right to maintain that the human mind does not work exactly like a serial and binary computer. He is also correct to argue that top-down, rule-based syntactic programming is not the way to achieve practical machine intelligence. This, however, in no way proves that his scenario establishes that computer thinking/understanding/intelligence is impossible.

PRINT THIS!

Searle's counterfactual founders on its centrepiece – the possibility of creating a Leviathantine template-response database that could in principle provide for every conversational contingency.

Exceeding the computational capacity of all and any devices that could be manufactured in our universe, its dimensions and thus the time required for scanning and retrieval are for all purposes infinite. As a consequence, the only thing that *does* follow from Searle's premises is that no one could ever write down all answers to all TT interactions and stuff them in boxes, which we knew anyway.

The thought experimenter presupposes that any question that can be formulated can be fed into the Chinese Room, which will then dish out the correct answer. Conceptually, this is equivalent to writing down every line of every book that could ever be written and stuffing them in boxes, indexed for retrieval. To bring out the true dimension of this supertask, forget all the books that could be crammed into the Chinese Room Larger Than The Universe. Let us look at just *one* book, and a pint-sized one at that: two hundred pages, fifty lines per page, fifty spaces per line.

Numerically, the problem consists of calculating the state space for our pocket book. The amount of all possible printable spaces in it is $200 \times 50 \times 50 = 500,000$. The variables with which every printing space can be filled are the lower and uppercase letters of the alphabet plus the typographical signs. To keep things simple, let us agree that there are only fifty signs in all: twenty-four lowercase, twenty-four uppercase, plus the period and the comma. The number of possible permutations? A number so vast that it is in almost every sense meaningless: $50^{500,000}$.

Here is why. The number of atoms in the universe is 10^{80}. The universe itself has been around for fourteen billion years. Assuming that every atom is a printing press, and that each has been printing non-stop since the Big Bang at the rate of atomic vibrations, by now they would have printed such a minute fraction of a single book in a single box on a single shelf that you would have to work your way through two hundred pages of zeros before, on the very last page, third line from the bottom, you would find the first meaningful decimal.

Print *this*!

Searle's counterfactual has exactly zero upshot for computer thinking. What it does rather well, on the other hand, is show that traditional top-down AI research is a dead end. For decades now, Douglas Lenat, perhaps the last of the old school, has tried to spawn artificial intelligence by spoon-feeding heaps of data to a program

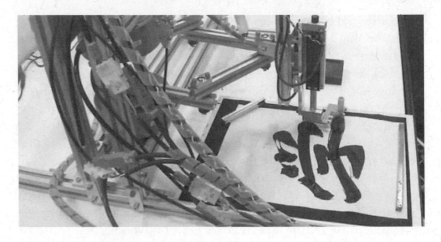

The thought experimenter presupposes that any question that can be formulated can be fed into the Chinese Room, which will then dish out the correct answer.

called CYC (as in en*cyc*lopedic). Among other quanta of intelligence about human consensus-reality – common-sense knowledge, in English – typed into the machine are such arcane morsels as "bread is food," "George Bush wears underpants," and "you're wet when you sweat."

At some point in the unspecified future, CYC is supposed to reach the saturation point, whereby it will become cognitively independent, whereupon it will spring into action and start to augment its knowledge database on its own – say, by reading books. Hope, of course, springs eternal. Meanwhile, not only AI gadflies but insiders concede that the top-down, syntax-based approach to machine thinking displays all the signs of a degenerating research program. Much as I predicted in 2000, here I go again: Lenat's crusade will fail to bring home the grail.

TROMPE L'OEIL

Searle's counterfactual is essentially a clever *trompe l'oeil*. Here is why. The philosopher invokes understanding as the criterion for deciding whether a TT player is truly intelligent rather than only looking like he is. For all I know, however, Searle does not understand his own arguments. For all I know, there is a homunculus in his cranium that mindlessly shuffles molecules from one place to another in accordance with a mindless if tremendously long program. Undeniably, this elaborate shuffling gives a semblance of purposeful behaviour to the walking and talking constellation of atoms that, for convenience's sake, we refer to as John Searle.

But underneath the façade, there are only trillions of particles of inert matter and a lone demon that agitates them according to instructions coded in the language of physics and biochemistry. In short, contrary to all appearances, Searle does not understand what he says, and only the phenomenal velocity of the homunculus's operations perpetrates the hocus-pocus of reasoned response, i.e., of intelligence. Amused but not convinced? Then try to prove me wrong. Try as hard as you can, you cannot – at least, in Searle's terms. To prove *me* wrong, you would have to prove *him* wrong.

Let us look at the whole set-up from another angle. The occupant of the Chinese Room is said not to understand the squiggles and squoggles which he can, nevertheless, manipulate expertly according to the transformation rules written down in his rule-book. My question is: How can Searle know that the occupant does not understand Chinese? Since he cannot look inside the man's head, the only sources for this claim must be functional and behavioural in nature. Once again, Searle buys into the very premise he would like to reject.

Suppose that, to prove his point, the philosopher locks himself in the room. After all, he *knows* that he does not understand Chinese. No dice, either, for how do I know that he really does not understand Chinese? My sole source of evidence is his solemn oath or his behaviour, both of which amount to the same thing: inductive functionalism. After all, even if we were to crack his head open, we would not discover "understanding," only a mindless swirl of atoms and molecules.

Like it or not, once more Searle's argument relies on the very premise he wishes to undermine. This is no accident, simply because it is impossible to understand "understanding" in any other terms than its actual use. Try this at home. Ask yourself whether you understand that $2 + 2 = 4$. Presumably your answer is affirmative. Now, prove that you understand it in any manner that does not involve manipulating the elements of the equation or, more generally, interacting with the real world in a manner consistent with the fact that you understand it. Try as hard as you can, you can't.

Knocked out again, the sceptic could remix the Chinese Room into yet another argument that goes like this. Assuming that the man in the room does not understand Chinese – in other words, assuming what is to be established – the mental phenomenon of "understanding" is not contained in his head. Nor is it contained in any one of the bits of paper that store the rules or the answers. Since none of the constitutive elements understands anything, the person-plus-paper cannot understand anything either, no matter how many more rules and bits of paper are fed into it. After all, if one scrap of paper does not think, two scraps do not either, nor do three, four, or any higher number. Right?

Wrong. To see why, consider Searle's own brain. Take any small part of it, be it a dendrite or even any of the proteins from which it is constructed, and ask yourself whether it understands anything. Of course, it does not. Then take another part and ask the same question, and so on. As no one part of the brain understands any-thing, a mere expansion of non-understanding bits of brain in his head could not at any point give rise to intelligence, right? Which proves my point again: John Searle does not understand what he says.

LIKE THE POPE

Searle himself is a living *reductio* of his argument against con-sciousness. But even if you were to take his argument on face value, you would end up in the land of Oz. For one, in Searle's world there would be no rivers. A river is, after all, but an agglomeration of droplets swirling and twirling around one another. But as no one droplet carries the quality of riverness, where is the river? Where are streams, oceans, and soups in the world where stream-ness, oceanness, and soupness are not localized in any of their con-stitutive elements?

Let us do it again in slow-mo. Rivers, oceans, and soups emerge from agglomerations of droplets or, deep down, H_2O molecules. No one droplet or molecule triggers any kind of phase-transition from a mere collection of river droplets into a full-blown river. Yet, to be consistent, Searle cannot speak of rivers because riverness is an emergent property that does not reside in its constitutive com-ponents – just as thinking does not reside in the properties of the atoms that build neurons in a brain or chips in a computer.

Not convinced? Here is another *reductio*, this time constructed along diachronic lines. The sceptic maintains that no blind, mindless, unconscious, information-recombinant process could give rise to mentality and semantics. But once again he himself constitutes the best proof to the contrary, inasmuch as, just like all of us, he is the product of a blind, mindless, unconscious, and information-recombinant process: evolution.

Watching John Searle get knocked out time and time again, only to dust himself off and continue the skirmish, you may begin to sense a deeper methodological problem. There is simply no evidence on earth that could ever prove to his satisfaction that he is not an adroit android. After all, no matter how smart a person or a machine is, you can *always* insist that deep down it is all a matter of mere programming. And so Searle insists that no program could ever think, even as his doubts are no longer scientific but dogmatic since they cannot be falsified. At this point the sceptic becomes not only irrefutable but infallible, like the pope.

In an essay entitled "The Mystery of the Chinese Room," from a 1996 collection entitled, appropriately enough, *The Mystery of the Chinese Room*, Lem himself countered Searle's thought experiment with one of his own. Take a jigsaw puzzle, proposes the writer, reverse all the tiles blank side up and mix them up thoroughly. Then bring someone into the Jigsaw Room and ask him to assemble the puzzle still blank side up, going entirely by the contours (read: formal features) of the tiles. Once you turn the solved puzzle over, of course, you discover an answer to a TT-type question.

That is all. Now ask yourself: Does the Jigsaw Room scenario prove anything about the impossibility of computer intelligence? If you answer "No, how could it?" you have also answered Searle, just because Lem's scenario is wholly isomorphic with the Chinese Room. Caustically, Lem himself observes that the latter precludes Artificial Intelligence as much as a refutation written in chocolate éclairs precludes the next volcanic eruption of Mount Etna.

A BEVY OF PIGEONS

In *The Symbolic Species* (1997), anthropologist Terrence Deacon entertained an even wackier variation on the Chinese Room by replacing the man with a bevy of pigeons. Each bird had been miraculously trained to match incoming Chinese characters to those in the rule book and, subsequently, to those in the storage boxes. Even though no single pigeon could be charged with knowing Chinese, concludes the author, collectively they would be language processing.

This is correct. But what follows? It is difficult to tell. At this point the counterfactual has become so outlandish that the only vision it conjures in my mind is that of aeons needed to train gazillions of birds to process the variable input of some five thousand characters in the Chinese language. This is not to even mention that most ideograms are neologistically recombinable, mooting the scenario from the outset – unless, of course, you bring a Chinese-speaking pigeon trainer into the room or allow that the birds could learn Chinese as they went along. QED.

All this is to say that, more than the infinitely large cosmos filled with pigeons, feathers, birdseed, birdshit, and people trying to have a conversation with them by means of bits of paper, I would find it more plausible that, over aeons of habitat pressure, the birds themselves would evolve into a thinking species with as much fluency in Chinese as the Chinese. Perhaps recognizing this, Deacon claims not so much to furnish a rigorous answer to "Are the birds in the Chinese Room thinking or not?" as to highlight the gulf between indexical (syntactic) and symbolic (semantic) operations.

You might be justified in concluding at this point that the Turing test is really a Rorschach test by another name, inasmuch as everyone seems to see in it what they want to see. If so, let me put my cards on the table. I regard the entire Chinese Room diatribe as to whether computers can *really* think or *merely* process information satisficingly enough to get along in the world to be meaningless in Turing's sense – semantically not empty, but pointless and sterile. Like love, consciousness is not a localizable *object* that can be put on display but is instead a *process* detectable by its effects. It is a manner of describing a manner of behaving.

Whether computers can ever understand a story they have just read or written is an empirical question to be resolved by future generations of people and machines. Naturally, pragmatic factors such as socio-cultural traditions or even legislation may come between us and an acknowledgment of thinking in machines for no other reasons than that they are machines. Bear in mind, however, that the ability to function in the world – one part of which is communication with other thinking beings – has always been sufficient grounds for ascribing intentionality (or derived intentionality, if the term is not tautological in this context) in humans by humans.

NO MORE, NO LESS

In *I Am a Strange Loop* (2007), Hofstadter concludes that Searle's error stems from assuming that "the level of the most primordial physical components of a brain must *also* be the level at which the brain's most complex and elusive mental properties reside."[2] This is an elegant exposition of what is known in the parlance as a systems argument. Even though the man inside the Chinese Room really does not understand Chinese, the system as a whole acts in a manner that is indistinguishable from someone who does. The view that the mind is nothing but a kind of software running on cranial hardware is, of course, a textbook case of material reductionism.

But where does the mind come from? Like Turing, Hofstadter regards the question as misconceived, and in an effort to illustrate why, he elaborates the idea formulated more than half a century ago by Herbert Simon and Allen Newall, that intelligence consists of the ability to manipulate multiple levels of symbolic structures.[3] In a whimsical analogy to thermodynamics and statistical mechanics – two equivalent but mutually non-reducible levels of description of physical systems – Hofstadter describes consciousness in terms to two different levels: thinkodynamics, at the neuronal and synaptic level, and statistical mentalics, at the level of symbolic operations.

At the level of which we are aware, the mental pictures in our minds – be it sorrow at the passing of one's uncle or satisfaction at being accepted into grad school – ignore microscopic elements such as neurotransmitters firing, synapses activating, and so on. Naturally, all mental pictures are at bottom no more than the sum total of small-scale events that are purely physical and intentionless. And in between are the countless biophysical processes and countless levels of organization that, gradually, represent any given input more and more symbolically, i.e., mentally.

There is no unique "Eureka" level where it all comes together as a mind that is separate from all the other levels, just as there is no unique moment in human ontogeny when a child begins to think or a moment of phase transition when a stream turns into a river. There are only increasingly complex symbolic representations of neural activity, at least one of which – the one we are aware of – contains models of other subsystems and thus ingrates the "self." So what is the mind? It is a dance of non-isomorphic levels of description. It is a non-local epiphenomenon. It is an attribution made possible by Theory of Mind in other minds.

The last word on where the mind comes from goes, appropriately enough, to Turing. In his magisterial *The Essential Turing* (2004), Jack B. Copeland, director of the Turing Archive for the History of Computing, refers to Turing's lost proof that has a direct bearing on the apparent mind-brain duality. Stunningly, Turing appears to have proven that, through the process of learning, initially random neural networks could self-organize into a "universal Turing machine with a given storage capacity."[4]

The implications for the apparent duality – from top-down, minds and complex symbolic sequential processing; from bottom-up, parallel cascades of firing neurons – are not hard to tease out. If correct, Turing's proof established that the human brain can be modelled as a universal computer running on a bioneural network. Here then is the long-sought synthesis of the top-down and bottom-up perspectives. Deep down, the more-or-less continuous and coherent source of memory and self-awareness that we call the mind is a neural network organized from discrete events of the brain. No more, no less.

DICTY

Let us come back one last time to Searle and his riverless world. His claim that computers cannot ever evolve mentality amounts to claiming that there are no such things as autocatalytic properties. This is a mystifying position in view of the large and growing body of research on autocatalytic systems, spearheaded by Stuart Kauffman. Decades-long in the making, his findings open a Sesame of scientific treasures of which we may yet have caught but a glimpse, precisely because they are so fundamental in nature, being abstracted from any specific physical embodiment.

Kauffman set out to investigate the characteristics of complex networks irrespective of what they were made of: neurons, genes, transistors, light bulbs, phone relays, and so on. His insight was that there may be some fundamental properties common to all systems that inhere in their level of complexity and not in their material characteristics – properties that obtain as much for the Amazon as for rivers of sand cascading down Baltic dunes, or for cascades of firings in a connectionist network in our brain or inside a biterary computhor.

Varying input levels between neighbouring elements of networks, he stumbled on something extraordinary. Tucked away between a degenerative level, where the net would sputter into a steady state, and the onset of chaos, where stable patterns were as hard to detect as in a table of random numbers, there was a narrow band with a strikingly different behaviour. The instant you hit it, the network would come alive. Instead of doing nothing all, frozen solid for all eternity, or cranking up blizzards of "snow," it would cycle through a rich but limited number of states.

Buried among all possible configurations, there was a range that was dramatically different: not chaotic or rigidly ordered but complex. And, if that were not amazing enough, far from being a freaky anomaly, for *any* network there was always at least one auto-catalytic optimum between degeneration and chaos. Emergence, it turns out, is only waiting to emerge in all kinds of places, often suddenly, in what is known as a phase transition: a rapid onset of novel properties throughout the system, such as when water freezes into ice. Watch the water drain next time you take a bath. Once the level drops – bang, all of a sudden you get a mini-whirlpool funnelling into the drain.

The point is that water (or air) turbulence cannot be explained in terms of its individual components. The behaviour of the emergent state is absolutely unpredictable from the initial settings. You can explain viscosity or density in terms of the properties of molecular H_2O, but not turbulence. Put differently, fluid dynamics can model the vortex *motion* but not its *onset*. Like intelligence, turbulence emerges only at a certain level of system complexity without being detectable in any way prior.

So it is with esprit de corps, which emerges only at the level of a social group and is not derivable from or reducible to the characteristics of the human "atoms." Traffic fatalities are globally predictable to within a margin of error, reliably making money for the insurers. But at the level of a single accident, there is nothing to indicate death *rates*, even though statistical regularities emerge from lower-level collisions.

Kauffman set out to investigate the characteristics of complex networks irre-spective of what they were made of: neurons, genes, transistors, light bulbs, phone relays, and so on. His insight was that there may be some fundamen-tal properties common to all systems that inhere in their level of complexity and not in their material characteristics – properties that obtain as much for the Amazon as for rivers of sand cascading down Baltic dunes, or for cas-cades of firings in a connectionist network in our brain or inside a biterary computhor.

The same phenomenon shows up in Dicty (*Dictyostelium discoi-deum*), in many ways a garden-variety amoeba. In distress situations, however, this monocellular protozoan behaves in a way that is noth-ing short of remarkable: it begins to aggregate and act like a super-organism, even though it lacks a central "brain." Yet, until it reaches this state, there is nothing to hint of this dramatically novel behaviour. In a similar way, termites construct their mounds with perfect meridian alignment and dynamic-airflow air-conditioning, without blueprints or an architect-in-chief. Study each worker as much as you please, however, and you will not find a mini-compass or air-con module in its brain.

Many complex systems, in short, display emergent properties, which is another way of saying that many complex systems are self-organizing. We can know about them as much as there is to know, and we will still not be able to derive their higher-level autocatalytic properties. And so it is with thinking. Below deck, human beings run in accordance with blind, inanimate, inflexible laws: Pauli's exclusion principle, Ohm's law, and so on. But even though this deterministic rule-book is always there, it manifestly does not stand in the way of emergence of higher-lever properties such as mentality or volition.

After all, we all think – which is to say, we all assume we all do.

OPERATIONAL DEFINITION?

One would expect little consensus among the opponents and proponents of the TT on its extension and validity. It is striking, however, how little consensus there is even on such a fundamental issue as to what the TT actually tests for. Thinking? Computer thinking? Equivalence of computer and human thinking? Their identity? Take any two philosophers writing on the subject, and the odds are they will be as far apart as Robert French and Dale Jacquette, for whom the test defines, respectively, intelligence and *artificial* intelligence.

Among this plethora of positions and oppositions, the only one that has rallied philosophers over the decades is the belief that the TT is an operational definition of whatever it is supposed to define. P.H. Millar was explicit on this point, declaring that the TT gives "an operational definition" of – judging from his context – computer thinking. Ned Block, of the "blockhead" counter, calls it a "behaviourist definition of intelligence." Even Turing's assiduous biographer Andrew Hodges categorizes it as "an operational definition of 'thinking.'"[5]

The misunderstanding persists all the way into the twenty-first century. In a retrospective on the first fifty years of the TT, Robert French declares that the test was proposed as an "operational definition of intelligence." In the Wadsworth Philosophers Series, John Prager goes as far as to underscore his belief that the TT is an "*operational definition* by which the performance of a machine could be compared with that of a human at tasks presumed to require intelligence."[6]

Why is this a misinterpretation? First of all, because it fundamentally misrepresents Turing's view of what the test was all about. This view was so important to him that, in the very first sentence he uttered on the 1952 BBC panel on artificial intelligence, he objected, "I don't want to give a definition of thinking."[7] Secondly, it is perfectly possible for a machine to think as well as you and I do and still fail the test – just as people hampered with mental handicaps, linguistic impediments (for example, dyslexia), or massive cultural differences could flunk it. As such, if the test gives a definition of thinking, it is a deeply flawed definition to start with.

In truth, if all that the TT does is give an operational definition of a new concept, then the definition itself needs little justification but the test becomes of scant interest and consequence. In my opinion, it is just the reverse. The test cashes out the concept of machine thinking by appealing to our ordinary notion of thinking, however fuzzy it might be. In fact, it provokes so much gut-level hostility precisely because of the appreciable overlap between normal human thinking and the behavioural potential of a computer.

An unequivocal sign that Turing thought of the test in inductive rather than logical-categorical terms is the pragmatic stance he adopts in "Computing Machinery and Intelligence." In the central passage, he states that by the year 2000, "we will be able to speak of machines thinking without expecting to be contradicted."[8] By the same token, he never claims that a computer that aced the TT would think. In fact, he regards such a proposition as meaningless. It is for no other reason that he *replaces* the question "Can machines think?" with the TT. Any interpretation of the test as an operational definition of computer thinking would presumably strike him as equally meaningless.

Mapping computer thinking onto the semantic evolution of the concept, the TT does not provide the necessary or sufficient conditions for machine thinking. Its merits lie, instead, in providing a source of controlled *inductive* evidence for or against computer intelligence. And with this goal in mind, it can be retooled into as exacting an examination as need be. One limitation of the TT brought up by sundry critics is its inability to test the non-verbal aspect of the players' behaviour. Although true, the limitation can be easily remedied. Non-verbal behaviour can be described by the players, and examiners can and should demand descriptions of complex activities on the order of planning a lecture, reconciling quarrelsome friends, selecting a prom date, and such like.

FLUGBLOGS

Strangely enough, one might amass heaps of evidence that a computer thinks as well as you and I do, and it might still fail to impersonate a human being in a suitably rigged examination. In "Subcognition and the Limits of the Turing Test" (1990), Robert French describes, in fact, an entire class of protocols devised to trip the machine. Whether they remain the kind of tests that Turing had in mind is another story.

French analyzes a range of tricks that could identify a machine owing to the fact that human minds are primed for subcognitive associations. A good illustration of the latter comes from the so-called Rating Games, which can involve different categories such as neologisms, jokes, and advertisements. For example, players may be asked to rate, on the scale of 0 (completely implausible) to 10 (completely plausible):

* "Flugblogs" as the name Kellogg's would give to a new breakfast cereal;
* "Flugblogs" as the name of a new computer company;
* "Flugblogs" as the name of big, air-filled bags worn on the feet and used to walk on water.[9]

The key to detecting a machine is a significant modification of the STT. French assumes that he could poll a statistically viable sample of people on the Rating Games prior to the test and use the results during the actual run to make out the computer. The participant whose answers matched the statistical profile would likely be human, who, in rating the entries, would automatically fall back on subcognitive associations typical of beings who experience the world in the same way the rest of us do.

This is true. As we continuously discover, many facets of what we used to regard as cognitive (deliberate) processing is really sub-

cognitive. The recent discovery of mirror neurons is a paradigmatic case. Although we have no idea how they do it, mirror neurons
recognize and respond not to gestures but to the *intentions* behind
the gestures of other agents. In this, they are part and parcel of the
suite of biological adaptations known as Theory of Mind that
enable us to recognize agency and, as such, enable human-type
communication.

French's wedge test is grounded in the fact that, when information is scarce, we fall back on quick and dirty guesstimates. As a
result, we may get things wrong, but even when we do, we get them
consistently wrong. This is precisely why anchoring effects can be
used to drive a wedge between human and computer. A machine
like Watson would likely know the answer to "How many African
countries are in the UN?" but if it did not, it would presumably not
be primed to guesstimate it as humans are.

In short, to pass the wedge test, computers would have to exhibit the same subcognitive effects as people do. Or would they? Some
people always score as outliers, casting some doubt on French's
stratagem. But even if that were not the case, my question is, so
what? Even if you could guess that one player is a computer, that
would tell you nothing about whether it is thinking. Moreover, as
we move toward connectionist nets and more flexible, learning-
based interactions with their environment, the premise loses some
of its bite. It runs out of steam even further in systems that might
be capable of learning and experiencing the world in ways similar
to humans, such as biterary computhors of the *cis-humana* type.

In sum, the ability to think is best appreciated in terms of an
inductive theory about an interactant's ability to function in ways
that are *intelligible to* humans but not necessarily in ways that are
indistinguishable from humans. Once again, if we ever find ourselves
face to face with a computer that could ace the Turing test, we will
find it unnecessary to run one. The inductive evidence from daily
intercourse with the machine will be far in excess of the evidence
needed to resolve whether it can be said to think.

ON BEING MENTAL

Needless to say – but perhaps worth saying all the same – all of my
arguments are grounded in the physicalist concept of mind. Without
getting entangled in the long history of division between dualists and

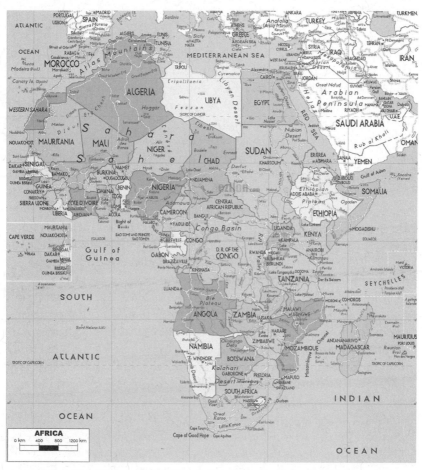

A machine like Watson would likely know the answer to "How many African countries are in the UN?" but if it did not, it would presumably not be primed to guesstimate it as humans are.

materialists, it simply means that they are grounded in the non-Cartesian school of thought in which mind and consciousness are a part of physical reality, not apart from it. Historically, of course, this has not been the only view in town. In the twentieth century alone, philosophers and scientists as diverse as Bergson, Elsässer, and Polanyi insisted on a vitalist component (*élan vital*) in all living organisms.

On their view, computers by definition could never become thinking or alive. An essentialist could always maintain that a machine that passed the TT only mimicked human thinking rather than duplicated it. If I am unconvinced by this type of objection, it is because the difference between mimicking some action and duplicating is fluid at best. Take a machine that finds logical proofs, regulates traffic, diagnoses diseases, and beats grandmasters at chess. Such systems exist today, but it would make little sense to say that they only mimic all these actions.

There exist, of course, scores of refutations of vitalist arguments, most of which follow from the refutation of Descartes' analysis of the mind-body problem – in effect denying the duality. Among those, Donald Davidson's is arguably the most original, if only because it stands the duality on its head by arguing that intentionality provides an argument *against* dualism. Indeed, his so-called anomalous monism amounts to claiming that instead of two kinds of stuff in the world, mental and physical, there is only one, which we conceptualize in these complementary ways.

Curiously enough, anti-dualist arguments have also emerged from the philosophical antipodes under the name of panpsychism. Panpsychists even start from the same premise as physicalists, namely that brains are minds, thus dispensing with *élan vital* and other animistic additives. At bottom, in other words, both physicalists and panpsychists see everything in the world as the interplay of physical forces and their manifestations: elementary particles, chemical molecules, rocks and rivers, livers and brains. But panpsychists take the other fork in the road when it comes to consciousness.

The standard problem for the physicalist is how to get from colours and flavours of inanimate quarks to the subjective visual or gustatory sensations of a mind in human beings like you and me. Panpsychism offers a solution – and it is a drastic one. It cuts through the Gordian knot by postulating that everything in the universe is imbued with mentality and subjectivity. Nuts, you say? Well, yes. On the other hand, if even subatomic particles have proto-mentality, the problem of getting from brains to minds disappears in a flash.

The problem is, if all matter in the cosmos is psychic, everything that is matter should have psyche embedded in it. Do Weakly Interacting Massive Particles (WIMPs) and Massive Compact Halo Objects (MACHOs), then, desire to avoid solo existence as they gravitationally attract one another? Are neutrinos mental hermits that elect to interact so weakly as to be almost undetectable? Do molecules bond to live happily ever after? Do electrons dream of electric sheep? Panpsychists' defence that the mentality of elementary particles is so vestigial that it goes unnoticed begs the question of how they know it is there in the first place.

In another version, the same panpsychism said to permeate all natural bodies excludes man-made artifacts and objects such as rocks or planets, which are said to lack the unity of organization. If both exceptions look suspiciously like Ptolemaic epicycles, it is because crystal lattices in rocks such as quartz, the second most profuse mineral in our planet's crust, are uniformly organized. Moreover, atoms are immutable and, as such, should preserve their volitional properties even if they migrate from natural hair to artificial hair extensions.

Indeed, if you think about it, any version of panpsychism that embraces such a radical discontinuity between different types of atoms or objects – some volitional, others not – is really physicalism by another name. At some stage in the universe, mentality appears where it was not there before, so panpsychism is stuck with the same emergence problem as physicalism. Not surprisingly, panpsychism is hardly a major school of thought in philosophy, to say nothing of science. It accuses physicalism of being at odds with experience and reality, be it commonsensical and scientific, yet neither folk physicists nor those gainfully employed at CERN have ever reported running into stones that would refuse to break bones or muons giving the finger to the magnets that drive them. Add to this the problem of explaining what exactly is the mentality of a quark, or the combination problem (how does human mentality emerge from the combined mentalities of atoms?), and you can safely lay panpsychism to rest.

7

ToM

Kismet; PaPeRo; Guilty as Charged; Eureka; Meaning;
Elementary, Dear Wason; Biology in Action; Driving Range;
Insula Cortex; On Being Redundant

KISMET

Both Kismet and I are clever contraptions that excel in social interactions. But whereas I am an assembly of colloids and dendrites,
Kismet is a heap of gears and microchips. To the world it presents
a vaguely donkey-like physiognomy with oversized eyes, furry eye-
brows, pointy ears, and a pair of orange lips that look like they were
squeezed out of a tube of novelty-store toothpaste. In short, not
much in human or even humanoid terms. And yet, unfailingly, this
coarse configuration of extensible parts is integrated as a face with
all that it implies in psychological terms.

One reason is its surprising mobility. The steel-mounted elements
are capable of assuming a variety of shapes identifiable as expressions of surprise, delight, disgust, or doubt. Moreover, this MIT robot is more than a one-trick donkey. It is equipped with synthetic
speech which allows it to engage in basic chatter and even learn a
limited amount of new words, such as people's names. Six cameras
allow it to track its environment and focus on visitors' faces or on
objects they may brandish in front of its eyes.

At the end of the day, it has, of course, as much personality as a
New York subway turnstile. Yet children love to play with it, seemingly oblivious to the fact that Kismet is an aggregate of steel and
circuits – a mechanical puppet on binary strings. Shyly at first, they
might show the robot their favourite toys and see the gesture
acknowledged with a nod and a toothpaste grin. Ice broken, they

might scamper around trying to dress up their new friend or convince it to play a game, while Kismet obligingly turns the smiley
donkey face to follow the commotion. All the while, the kids chirp
to it relentlessly, peering at its face and in general treating it like a
living pet.

Odd as it may seem, there is nothing odd in any aspect of the
children's behaviour, down to the fact of looking into the robot's
eyes. The naturalness of this gesture is confirmed by Juan-Carlos
Gomez's research with apes, who also frequently look into humans'
eyes when issuing requests. This shows not only that apes monitor our
attentional state but suggests that they may be aware that intentionality originates behind the eyes and not in the limbs that carry out the
requested action, be it dispensing food, playing, or grooming.

Returning the attention, Kismet learns and speaks out the children's names, making the illusion of communicating and developing a relationship even more seductive. Indeed, the impression of
interacting with another mind is so natural that it is shamelessly
exploited in bestselling toys like Furbies and in the latest generations of Japanese robotic pets for the elderly which speak gibberish
until they "learn" simple expressions from their owners. In reality,
they automatically begin to speak a certain number of phrases after
a factory-preset time.

Today Kismet gathers dust on a display stand at the MIT museum in Cambridge, Massachusetts. But in its heyday in the late
1990s, it was such an interactive sensation that even roboticist
Rodney Brooks did not hesitate to hyperbolize, "Kismet is alive.
Or may as well be. People treat it that way."[1] Certainly most children did, seeing the robot as a friend that liked them back, even
though they were carefully told that it was not alive but only programmed to respond to verbal and visual cues. But if you think
that only kids could be taken in by such crude plays, you are due
for a rethink.

PAPERO

Meet Ed Feigenbaum, distinguished AI expert, whose name you
may recall from the Feigenbaum test, the *Jeopardy*-type domain-
specific imitation of the Turing test. If there is one individual who
ought never to fall prey to robotic mimicry, it is he. Feigenbaum
recalls spending a part of the day with PaPeRo (for Partner Pet

Robot) – a social-interactive machine of the sort that the Japanese excel in – on a visit to the artificial intelligence labs of NEC (Nippon Electric Company) in Tokyo a few years ago. His stunned reaction is worth quoting in full:

> When I saw they booked me for an hour with PaPeRo, I thought I would be bored to tears after twenty minutes. But that was not the case. The experience was riveting, fascinating, attention-grabbing. How could that be? PaPeRo was just a bunch of plastic and electronics running around the floor, and I knew how it worked, so there was no magic.[2]

No magic – but enchantment all the same. The diminutive robot was evidently expert at playing a playful, lovable child, tapping into the adaptive psychosocial mechanisms embedded in all of us. You may remember the late Steve Jobs's animated film company Pixar and their skits depicting two desk lamps. America or Asia, male or female, young or old, the whole world saw the same thing. The baby lamp was cute and playful, the mommy lamp was loving and protective. All this about two inarticulate pieces of standard-issue office equipment hopping about.

Things are no different with interactive software, beginning notably with Weizenbaum's binary therapist ELIZA. Named after Eliza Doolittle, a Pygmalionesque handiwork of a linguist Professor 'Iggins (if you remember your Shaw), the program was developed in the 1960s to imitate person-centred psychotherapy in the Rogerian tradition. The distinction is significant in that in this non-directive approach, tailor-made for computers, the therapist trades active probing for gentle prodding.

The goal is to create a non-judgmental environment that will give the patient unconditional positive feedback. In practical terms, the cyber-therapist invites the patient to monologue, from time to time coaxing progress with a thoughtful – or, if you like, thoughtless – "I see." When introspection stalls, it may be reactivated by turning statements verbatim into questions ("I lost it all." "You lost it all?") or by falling back on preset gambits such as "What does it suggest to you?" or "How did that make you feel?" When the session begins to show signs of sputtering out, the script rolls out the heavy arty: "Tell me about your childhood/mother/father/dreams."

No magic – but enchantment all the same.

The first casualty was Weisenbaum's assistant, who naturally knew only too well how the code was developed to mimic a knowledge-able therapist. All the same, once the script was up and running, she succumbed to the illusion that she was conversing with an understanding and sympathetic mind. After only a few minutes' typed interaction with the program, she got sufficiently involved to ask her incredulous boss to leave her alone with it.

She may have been the first, but she was not the last. Even as ELIZA was never meant to delude anyone that "she" could think and offer solace, like Nathanael West's hapless Miss Lonelyhearts she did so anyway, to her creator's perpetual exasperation. Today you can try a little therapy with dozens of online ELIZAs to find out how susceptible you are to the allure a perfectly unflappable shrink that, miracle of miracles, charges nothing by the hour. Or you can find an Easter egg in Apple Utilities that works more or less like the original, ready to lend an ear to your rants and sorrows.

Research shows that, as soon as machines are given a face and a voice, we are tempted to respond to them as if they had mentality. In literary studies, this propensity was recognized long before the science of psychology was even on the horizon. Known as pathetic fallacy, it is a matter of hanging human characteristics on inani-mate entities such as, for instance, the weather. The heavens crying raindrops over the heroine in distress may be the stuff of tacky melodrama, but it reveals a deep-seeded proclivity for Theory of Mind that goes beyond computers or even literature.

We all form bonds with old photos, mementos, heirlooms, and contexts ("they're playing *our* tune") that stir up our memories and emotions. In colonial North America, deprived of human contact for weeks if not months, *coureurs de bois* christened the machines that shared their daily toil: their rifles. Today's suburbanites fuss over their cars, New Agers talk to plants, Californians adopt their pets, Japanese marry virtual Nintendo girlfriends, and kids worldwide treat their teddies and dollies as if they were responsive and alive.

What gives?

GUILTY AS CHARGED

Stung by people's repeated failures to take ELIZA less seriously than they should have, Weisenbaum credited their readiness to project a mind where there was none to the fact that they did not understand computers. It takes a super-sceptical person, he wrote in *Computer Power and Human Reason*, to resist the temptation to anthropomorphize the machine's performance. Most people haven't the foggiest idea how algorithms work, and so they invariably bring to them "their model of their own capacity to think."[3]

In *Gödel, Escher, Bach*, Hofstadter adopted a similar stance, crediting our penchant for attributing minds to machines to gullibility. The implication is clear: AI experts like Weizenbaum's assistant or Ed Feigenbaum, versed in the intricacies of computer or algorithmic design, could never fall for ELIZA's or PaPeRo's cheap tricks. Obviously, such explanations do not explain anything, given the overwhelming evidence that we are primed to respond to facial and verbal cues as evidence of minds. Oscar Wilde's wisecrack about being able to resist everything except temptation – in this case, temptation to anthropomorphize robots, computers, and other inanimate entities – rings as true as ever.

Given that we are all guilty as charged, the big question is: Where is the source of this "guilt"? The answer is in one word, evolution, and in two and a half words: Theory of Mind (ToM). Our automatic projection of intentions onto the interactants we interact with is the work of a suite of evolved adaptations to detect minds, a must-have in such a highly social species as *Homo sapiens*. Turning the tables on Weizenbaum and Hofstadter, our mind-seeking and mind-seeing is not only perfectly natural in the biological sense but also, as we are discovering, it is the key to human-type communication.

Every normal person relies on being able to project mental states onto other beings and on having mental states attributed to oneself as part of making sense of one another's behaviour. So instinctive, so universal, and so successful is this process that it is clearly a domain-specific adaptation hard-wired into the brain rather than an incultured skill. Studies of apes, children, twins, and patients with chronic or acquired neural damage reveal the essential elements of its structure, as remarkable as they are commonplace.

The central aspect of ToM is our astonishing and astonishingly reliable ability to read people's minds – or, more precisely, to read minds off people's behavioural and linguistic cues. This ability is part and parcel of our everyday psychology by means of which we account for other folks' actions in terms of beliefs and desires. Each of us has our own little interaction engine-that-could, dedicated to detecting intentions in actions. Anything that meets its fairly primitive standards, from eye contact to pointing gestures, is primed to be apprehended as evidence of another mind.

In sum, more than a facilitator of human communication, ToM is actually its *enabler*. It enables us to perceive others, be they human, animal, or even machine, as intention-driven agents and as a result to frame what they do or say in terms of goals and purposes. If you have ever wondered why human communication is in general so effortless and effective, it is thanks to this instinctive private detector, always on the case, always sleuthing for verbal and non-verbal cues.

EUREKA

We love to share information about what we think and feel. But we succeed in doing so only thanks to the shared pre-sets for *intention* and *attention*. You and I could never communicate via this book if it were not for this prosocial pre-set and for the ToM module that enacts it. Together with the ability to appreciate each other as intentional agents, our ability to form a joint-attentional frame is the social-cognitive basis for our book-mediated "conversation" – and for all human communication, period.

The evidence from human ontogeny and primatology is compelling in this respect. Underscoring its fundamental role in our species, the capacity for mind-reading crystallizes in all normally developing infants as young as nine to twelve months old. As soon as they begin to point referentially, say, to their favourite toy, they keenly attend to the participating adult's grasp of what is going on, usually by means of eye contact. Strikingly, if the adult responds by showering them with attention but ignoring the toy, they persist in pointing to it. Do not attend to me, you big oaf, attend to what I want you to attend to!

Psychologist Michael Tomasello summarizes these findings thus:

> From almost as soon as they begin pointing infants understand the most important aspects of how human-style, cooperative communication works – they communicate on a mental level, within the context of common conceptual ground, and for cooperative motives – thus displaying something approaching the complete social-cognitive infrastructure of mature cooperative communication.[4]

But while infants acquire the ability to engage others mentally already in this prelinguistic phase, apes never develop it. They certainly do not lack the perceptional and motor skills to follow, for instance, the direction of a pointing finger. But they just do not get it. They see the finger and they follow its extension with their gaze, but no light bulb lights up in the Eureka moment when they ought to realize that it is meant to *mean* something. In contrast, in all ordinary one-year-olds this joint-intentional light bulb lights up without fail and brightly.

Significantly, apes are quite able to perceive other agents as intentionally motivated. Experiments demonstrate that they ably distinguish good-faith attempts thwarted by acts of God from situations in which somebody stiffs them for no reason. If there is a tasty morsel in a bucket that just keeps slipping out of the zoo-keeper's hands, the ape will wait patiently. But it will raise a ruckus if the keeper begins to hand it over and stops arbitrarily. Unable or unwilling? Our evolutionary cousins cope with this critical distinction very well. Manifestly, both apes and human infants recognize that agents have goals. Both grasp that agents strive to bring the state of the world closer to their internal (volitional) representations of it. Both recognize agents as rational, in the sense of making allowances for their motives. Unable? Okay. Unwilling? Time to hoot and display.

But this is where the parallels end. And this is precisely where human-level communication kicks in. Whereas the synchronization of joint attentions does not emerge in apes at all, in little people it emerges before the first year of age, never to fade away. Just think about it. Our everyday conversations are chock-full of apparent dead ends, such as:

"Wanna go out?
"My mom is sick."

We do not get logically or semantically from an invitation to a date to a parent's illness – and back. Except that in shared cultural space, it is tacitly understood that ill parents need attending to.

The operative word is "tacitly." There is absolutely nothing in this mini-dialogue to suggest how to flesh it out. We have to bring this knowledge from the outside, from the common background that enables this and an infinity of other social exchanges: verbal, gestural, or even wholly implicit. Where is the missing part of this exchange? In the context, obviously. But such context is never all-encompassing. Indeed, for practical reasons, it could not be. Instead, it is selected with a view to *what is reciprocally assumed to be relevant to a given conversation.*

It is Savile Row communication: we tailor not only the message but the context to fit the listener.

MEANING

Given the very structure of the communicative process – its inter-dependence, reciprocity, recursiveness, and reliance on explicit and tacit common ground – the assumption of shared intentionality, in itself deeply implicated in ToM, is the only one that makes sense of the whole set-up. Take even such a basic part of everyday conversation as irony. It entails stepping into each other's shoes to ensure that the message gets across. You monitor your friend's attention to see if she is getting it, your friend monitors yours to make sure she is getting what you want her to get, and vice versa.

The guiding principle behind this turning the tables on each other was first described by Paul Grice in a 1957 paper called "Meaning." Taking stock of what is going on when people communicate with each other, Grice homed in on intentions. He called them *reflexive* intentions, for the simple reason that they are intended to be recognized as having been intended to be recognized. A communication is successful if the meaning intended by the speaker (or writer) is identified by the listener (or reader) by recognizing the reflexive intention to express it.

Mind-reading is once again at the heart of the process, as it is in every communicative exchange, from water-cooler gossip to the baseball coach's pantomime to the Turing test. In all cases, participants have to parse for intentions to generate relevant inferences on the way to generating relevant conversational gambits. After all, generating only logically correct inferences is not enough. They may be correct but irrelevant – accurate but inadequate. Much like chessbots, chatbots need to prune their search space so that, instead of chasing all possible conversational gambits, they home in on the relevant ones (allowing that at times it may be relevant to be irrelevant, say, out of boredom, antipathy, or just whimsy).

If any aspect of conversation is non-algorithmic, it is being contextually relevant. The whole thing is analogous to the process whereby readers make inferences about what they read, just as you are doing right this very minute. We continuously and automatically flesh out what is printed on the page using empirical – or when needed, counter-empirical – assumptions about the world, guided by what we understand of the author's intentions. We do not need to be told, for instance, that people see with their eyes, that rain clouds carry rain, or that in Lem's most famous fiction, *Solaris*, an almost instantaneous travel between distant regions in space is possible. All this, and much more, are givens.

But at the same time we never invoke *all* possible inferences that could be inferred, most of which would be utterly beside the point. Think back for a moment to *La Chanson de Roland*. It is true that, like its author, its hero is a mammal which is viviparous, pneumo-branchiate, and placental. But make this point in your comparative-literature term paper and watch big question marks bloom on the margin just because your non sequitur contributes little of value to the appreciation of the epic qualities of the poem.

Analogously, when we converse with a machine during the Turing test, we want it to generate not only true but relevant commentary about whatever happens to be on the conversational menu. What does it mean for computhors? Do they need to develop ToM or only understand how it works? Do they need to develop emotions or only grasp the fundamental role they play in our lives? And how would we know computhors had emotions in the first place? Do machines that evince all signs of solace and consolation offer genuine solace and consolation or just indulge in gratuitous mimicry?

ELEMENTARY, DEAR WASON

Historically speaking, biology and then sociobiology directed their attention first to individuals and then to individuals in ecosystems, all the while grossly neglecting the features of individuals that enabled them to coexist with other individuals in collectives of individuals. Be that as it may, *Homo sapiens* is above all a social animal. Our natural habitat is not so much a savannah or a modern city as an assortment of blood kin, friends, and neighbours, themselves immersed in an ethnic or socio-cultural tribe at large.

Mutual aid, information sharing, and coordinated action are necessary even for our basic survival, not to mention that normal human psychological development hinges on being socially embedded. This is why our minds come pre-set for prosociality, ToM, emotional contagion, and other traits that, phylogenetically speaking, would not make sense in perennial hermits. This is why we are pre-tuned for identifying and evaluating facial expressions, postures, gestures, and behaviours in terms of mental states – for interpreting the external in terms of the internal.

These cognitive skills are ingrained in the subconscious, as they have to be in order to be so effortless and efficient. But subconscious effects can be teased out with the right wedge. Consider the notorious Wason test. Albeit not invented to test for evolved sociability, it does so anyway. At its heart lies a little brain-teaser that, framed in two vastly different ways, elicits vastly different results. In the abstract, the puzzle stumps almost everyone. But in the social form, as a narrative about detecting cheaters, it presents few problems. How could this be?

You can try this at home. Imagine four cards, each with a *number* on one side and a *colour* on the other. The particular cards in front of you display 5, 2, red, and black. The clue is this: *If you see an even number, the other side is red.* Now, what is the smallest number of cards you need to turn over to determine if the rule holds? Not so easy? Don't worry, even after reflection, most people get it wrong.

But now enter the world of people. For example, imagine that you are told, *If you use the car, you gotta fill the tank afterwards.* Makes sense, right? Now you face four cards that describe the following four situations:

Homer did not use the car.
Marge used the car.
Bart filled the tank.
Lisa did not fill the tank.

The question is exactly the same: what is the minimum number of cards you need to turn to spot free-riders? Elementary, dear Wason: the second and fourth cards, exactly the same as with the first problem.

In a similar vein, in 2005 Joseph Henrich et al. reported on a series of experiments around the world testing how deeply we have internalized norms for sharing and fairness. Their tool was the ur-experiment of prospect theorists/behavioural economists: the ultimatum game. One player is given a sum of money which he *must* split with another person whom he has never met before (and never does during the experiment). The game is played only once, with no possibility of collusion and no chance for cooperation evolving over time.

The trick is that the first participant makes a "take it or leave it" offer to the second player, who has only two options: assent or walk away from the deal. If the former, both keep whatever the split was. If the latter, both forfeit what was in the pot. According to classical economic theory, the whole thing is a no-brainer. Rationally, the first player should offer his absent accomplice only a token amount. As a utility maximizer, the other should accept the deal, since otherwise he gets zilch.

In real life, things look totally different, with players typically offering something like an even split. Indeed, offers where the first player keeps more than 60–70 per cent are almost universally rebuffed as unfair. The margin varies from culture to culture, and there are outliers who offer more than half as well as those who do not accept these overly generous splits, but the overall pattern is overwhelmingly that of fairness and reciprocity. We have internalized the norms very deeply indeed.

And the punchline? When people are told that they are playing against the computer, they immediately stop extending *and* rejecting one-sided offers. Instead, they play by the classical economics textbook: they try to maximize their take. It is just as I said: change the information available to the players, and you change the game itself.

BIOLOGY IN ACTION

What does this tell us about thinking computers? Human minds are primed to engage with minds – so much so that a pair of outsized eyes, a toothpaste grin, and especially an apparent ability to converse can generate an impression of a mind-like pattern. Minds are also primed to regard other minds differently from mindless entities. All the same, the TT exposes the limitations of a gut feeling that having a mind is an immanent property. In some contexts, whether a mind is really out there or whether it is only projected by a mind-seeking module is a distinction not worth making.

Although human minds are, naturally, always alive, life and sentience do not logically or even biologically entail each other. No need to look far for life without consciousness: plants provide a ready example. Those who would object to calling plants alive, even given the coordinated predatory activities of species such as Venus flytraps, would presumably acknowledge pleuromona (a kind of highly simplified bacteria), standard-issue bacteria, phages, or amoebas like Dicty. At the other end of the continuum we can meaningfully speak of consciousness sans life, presumably in computers and robots.

Seeing how grappling with the nature of consciousness is worse than grappling with a greased pig, you might think that conceptualizing life is a different story altogether – a hard biological, medical, or even forensic fact of the matter. Oddly enough, no one can say for sure what life is. Even as all extant definitions of life aim to carve nature at its joints, there is always some conceptual gristle or even meat left on the slab.

Understandably, most efforts go toward finding an intersection of traits presumed to be shared by all living organisms. One of the many scientists who pinned hopes on biochemistry was Norman John Berrill who, in his classic triple-decker *Biology in Action* (1966), ticked off fundamental functions such as growth, autonomous motion, metabolism, and self-replication as characteristic of life. In general, biologists tend to focus on prescriptions of shape and structure, metabolism of a range of chemical compounds, homeostatic adjustment to a changing environment, and sexual reproduction. As is to be expected, all are slanted towards carbon-based life.

The problem is that exceptions to these purportedly fundamental functions are not difficult to find, starting with viruses, worker bees (which cannot mate), or families of female-only wasps. There are two ways out of the bind. The first is to hang onto the conceptual core while papering over recalcitrant cases with a patchwork of ad hoc exceptions and conceptual epicycles. Certain variations or traits are ruled as inadmissible, with no generally acceptable justification for these decisions. Needless to say, machine life does not stand much chance of getting into the club.

The alternative is to shrug the biochemical slant altogether in favour of processes independent of organic composition and/or recombination. In most versions, these have to do with energy and information processing, structuring and organization, and emergence of coordinated response to the environment – as in the computer game *Life*, famously studied by John Conway (available online if you care to try it at home). By definition, the second approach

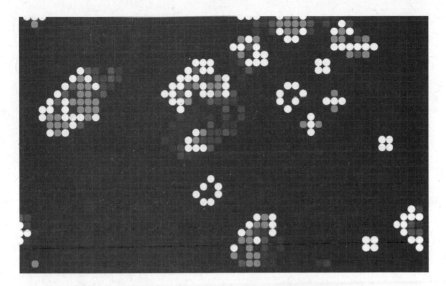

In most versions, these have to do with energy and information processing, structuring and organization, and emergence of coordinated response to the environment – as in the computer game Life, famously studied by John Conway (available online if you care to try it at home).

admits of life in computers as well as in still other life-forms, perhaps on one of the thousands of known exoplanets.

At the end of the day, everything depends on how anthropocentric and anthropomorphic we will choose to be in our future legal and medical statutes. Even as I type these words, computer life continues to be redefined as technology races on, much as life and death continue to be redefined in our own species. The term "clinical death," to take just one obvious example, did not exist until a few decades ago, acquiring reference only when the medical sciences secured a toehold in what used to be prohibited territory.

Where historically death was regarded as a monolithic cessation of life, the twentieth century has splintered the monolith. Now clinical death itself, defined as cardiac and pulmonary arrest (no heartbeat and no respiration), has been rendered obsolete by techniques and technologies ranging from CPR and life-support systems to epinephrine injections, defibrillators, and pacemakers. As a result, in the United States today, as per the Uniform Determination of Death Act, MDs and coroners pronounce "biological" or "brain" death defined by the cessation of all electrical activity in the brain.

DRIVING RANGE

The Nobel-winning neuroscientist Gerald Edelman has argued that thinking as we know it is the outcome of so many contingent processes and forces, including natural selection, morphological evolution, and biophysics, that it could never be embodied in a computer program. His argument is pellucid, his conclusions less so. Does Edelman suggest that computers could never think? Or only that computers could never think as humans do? The former is only an opinion, which, in my opinion, will be refuted by future developments. The latter is true, but so what? The RTT and Ulti-matest take care of that.

Generally speaking, people have a big advantage over machines insofar as people come preloaded with an instinctive grasp of how the basic physical and causal relations work in the world. This understanding permits us to operate with something like a Reality Principle, plugging the background into all kinds of tacit communicational contexts. But we have an even bigger advantage over machines: we want things, and we usually go after what we want. Computers, on the other hand, have no desires, including no desire to manipulate the world in a way that will bring it closer to their desires. In short, they have no volition.

Hence the big question: what will drive computhors? What will make them *want* to write novels or not want to write them? Emotions aside, biterary computhors will almost certainly have to have some form of algedonic control to build an internal hierarchy of preferences that will mimic rudimentary drives. The engineering aspect of this may be difficult, but the behavioural aspect is not. Unsecured energy supply, disruption (unplugging) or corruption (virus) of processing, and compromised integrity of the system would be tagged as negative. Continuance and more efficient tasking would go on the plus side of the program's ledger.

Surprisingly, John McCarthy, for decades a central figure in Artificial Intelligence (he coined the very name), speculated in 1990 that it will not "be advantageous to give programs the kind of motivational and emotional structure we have inherited from our ancestors."[5] This was the same McCarthy who had for a long time contended that the way toward machines who think was via machines with common sense. As every student of biology, ecology, and evolution knows, however, common sense does not develop in a vacuum.

This is precisely why, after decades of blundering in the desert, the so-called situated-AI school has come to realize that general intelligence must be embodied and embedded in the real world. Odd as it may sound, cognition is not just in our brain but is distributed all over the body and smeared all over the socio-cultural world around us. Intelligence is two-way traffic with feedback – the world impacts the evolving system and the evolving system impacts the world as it strives to survive. But what will make a computer strive to survive? What will make it want to want?

INSULA CORTEX

Much is said about the parallels between the cognitive sciences and cognitive psychology, relatively little about the parallels between artificial intelligence and evolutionary psychology. Molecular computing and genetic algorithms apart, much of evolutionary science is too imprecise to suit the programming formalism favoured in AI, and especially in American AI. It is no accident that the latter shunned fuzzy logic years after it had been put to work in Europe and Japan. This is unfortunate, since there is quite a bit to learn about intelligence from sociobiologists and evolutionary psychologists.

Human cognition is not entirely about rational deliberation, or not even mainly. Much of what we like to label "cognition" is really subcognition. To optimize performance, evolution has removed the awareness of most of the cognitive machinery it has bred in us so that we could get ahead in life without pausing to think about everything. As a result, the majority of human mental operations or processes are executed without deliberate reflection. To a large degree we are black boxes to ourselves.

Modularized subcognitive processing is in many ways the default mode of human brain power. At the same time, so much of our cognition is driven by emotion that to function effectively, we must function affectively. In what can rightly be described as a tectonic shift, emotions and feelings have finally over the course of the past twenty years been acknowledged as integral components of the machinery of thought and reason (in the process, emotions, or somatic affects, have also been distinguished from feelings, or mental representations of emotions).

As *biological* regulatory mechanisms, emotions could not have arisen in isolation from other life processes. They are implicated, in fact, in all kinds of adaptive behaviours, from mate-seeking and parenting down to thinking and decision-making. They keep us fixed on long-range goals and kick the somatic power train into overdrive in the presence of immediate stimuli. There is a time to reason and time to act, and when emotions grab the wheel, that time is now. Chemically mobilizing our minds and bodies, they tunnel our vision so that it fixates on the immediate consequences, regardless of what may come later.

This is not to say that emotions do the thinking or the decision-making for us. But, in a head-on collision with ultra-rational models of agency rooted in classical economic theory, emotions play a major role in cognition. In fact, as MRI scans of players in the ultimatum game graphically show, we often think in emotions. Unfair offers light up the insula cortex – the very area of the brain triggered by painful or malodorous stimuli – like a Times Square Christmas tree. Thinking about unreasonable splits, players are literally disgusted.

Just because emotions are underwritten by evolution, it does not mean that there is no cultural variation in how they are manifested. On the contrary, much of our emotional repertoire is mediated by communal rules of display. Also, like any other evolutionary mechanism, emotions can be adaptive in one set of circumstances and not at all in another. But, one way or another, they are there for a reason, and that reason has to do with driving the open-ended game of survival.

ON BEING REDUNDANT

Today's serial systems are critically vulnerable to external perturbations. Skip a few digits from the bitware, or a remove a few chips from the builtware, and you could as well drop the whole system from a plane sans parachute, the way it turns chaotic and churns out gibberish. The problem lies in the architectural and functional minimalism so prized by designers, which does not make room for redundancy and self-repair. This is in contrast to human brains, which are not only massively parallel but massively redundant in structure and operations. Naturally, this is also what makes human thinking so scattershot and far from always rational (though always capable of rationalizing).

If AI is to learn from evolution, we might need to revise our attitude to redundancy and stop banishing it in the name of performance optimization. If machines are to promote their own survival, they will almost certainly have to forego streamlining. Redundancy may need to be incorporated into the design as part of the homeostatic drive toward promoting resilience toward changes in internal and external environments. From the engineering standpoint, after all, our brains are anything but designed for maximum efficiency. Indeed, they could not be by the very biologic of evolution.

Brains may resemble general-purpose computers in their synaptic relays or in hard-wired modules being dedicated to running subroutines, but they are emphatically *not* what a traditional or even rational engineer would design. In place of fixed hierarchy, dedicated tasking, and optimized efficiency, there is a kilo and a half of neural jelly that is more redundant (or full of exaptations) than most people realize. Yet, in the real world, this bric-à-brac of suboptimal solutions outperforms the more compressed and efficient, but also more rigid and vulnerable, supercomputers.

Of the hundreds of examples of redundancy in our brains, perhaps the most evocative come from studies of brains that work anything but normally. An estimated 10 per cent of people with lesions in the vicinity of Wernicke's area display the type of verbal impairment (aphasia) typical of patients with damage in the physically discrete – although linked by nerve fibres – Broca's area. The inference is clear. There is partial overlap between the functions of these two areas which normally produce stunningly different types of aphasia. Broca's reduces verbal ability practically to zero. Wernicke's aphasics speak fluently and grammatically, but their speech amounts to semantic gibberish.

It is as if evolution invented packet switching before it was reinvented by human engineers to improve digital information transfer. Packet switching was a huge improvement over circuit switching – think back to the analogue telephone networks – which had to preserve the serial order of the transfer. When you speak with a friend over the phone, you sure want the beginning of the sentence to arrive before the end. Packet switching changed the need for linear order. On the Internet, data is disassembled into discrete packets and sent helter-skelter via any channel available. The payoff? Fantastic increase in reliability and speed: if any part of the network's bandwidth is filled to capacity, the packet can be relayed through another.

Redundancy is survival oriented. Tantalizingly, as became apparent during the first computer simulations of neural networks, it is also inbuilt into parallel processing. Back in 1954, a couple of MIT scientists trained a network of only 128 neurons to recognize patterns. Impressive as the feat was, they also stumbled on something potentially even more important. Random removal of up to 10 per cent of an already trained network had next to zero effect on its effectiveness. When it comes to "survivability," then, there is clearly nothing wrong, and a surprising lot right, with redundancy and neural nets.

8

Y2K+

Methuselah; Yes!; An Amphibian with a Stick; Ellipses in This Picture; Software for the Soul; Parallel Paradigm; Erlang and Mira; DelFlies; Eruntics; Cogito Paradox

METHUSELAH

In the day when biotech start-ups germinate like fungi, public relations spinners go to absurd lengths to brand their names with the public. Whatever they may lack in judgment they more than make up in hubris. Recently Human Genome Sciences enjoyed its fifteen minutes in the limelight with a prediction that by 2100 the sole causes of human death will be accidents, murder, and war. In other words, thanks to the yet-to-be-found wonders of regenerative medicine, old age, along with genetic degeneracy, will cease to be a lethal factor (cue in Louis Armstrong's "What a Wonderful World").

In a prospect as giddy as it is frightful, senility and mortality are to become "soluble" in our children's lifetime. And why not? Adam is said to have lived to 930 years, and Methuselah, the oldest man mentioned in the Bible, was 969 when he gave up the ghost. We are all dying to live longer and look younger, and the American Society for Aesthetic Plastic Surgery is only too eager to oblige. As their statistics show, every year America forks over billions of dollars to have some ten million fat deposits vacuumed, eyelids reshaped, noses redone, crow's feet and lips shot with Botox, big boobs reduced, droopy ones lifted, and all others beefed up with silicone.

Perhaps conditioned by their own advertising glitz and blitz, the media and even parts of the academic sector appear to have succumbed to the illusion that science and technology are like a year-round Christmas where, just as we tell little children, if we wish for something very much, it is going to happen. Unfortunately, this tendency, which without much exaggeration can be called wishful thinking, is particularly endemic among writers on computers in all their incarnations: Artificial Intelligence, robots, computational algorithms, the Internet, and so forth.

Their starting point is the indisputable fact that much of the world has become saturated with industrial machines, computers, telecommunications, and interactive information databases. This single trend is subjected to linear extrapolation, which is then used to underwrite one brave new scenario after another. And so since the 1950s a steady stream of wide-eyed hype has been promising not just automated but autonomous kitchens, smartly conversing robots, creatively thinking computers, general problem-solving software, self-evolving machines – all just round the corner or even already in full view.

How little has changed since then can be testified to by picking books on computers practically at random. Take one of the primers on electronic literature mentioned briefly in the introduction to this book. Without batting an eyelid, its author states that people in technologically advanced countries "are literally being reengineered through their interactions with computational devices." Literal hyperbole of this kind is, of course, nothing new. Back in 1983, one-time Pulitzer-winning science journalist Joel Shurkin chipped in from Cloud Nine that "most computer scientists now think that the Turing test is too easy,"[1] proving that Pulitzers ain't what they used to be.

Naturally, it is difficult in a single chapter to do justice to this global trend. And so, in what follows, I will confine my remarks to another blast from the past, Geoff Simons's *Are Computers Alive? Evolution and New Forms of Life* (1983). While utterly forgettable on its own merits, it is perfectly representative of the work of successive generations of techno-prophets who would pave the road to the future with the bodies of those who look askance at visions of crystal palaces of instrumental might. Its rhapsodic claims about technologies that to this day remain on AI's wish list deflate the bluster of present-day Nostradamuses better than any amount of reasoned critique could.

YES!

If best-selling science lite such as *Life on the Screen: Identity in the Age of the Internet* exemplifies hype in the 1990s, and if futurology lite such as *Beyond Human: Living with Robots and Cyborgs* exemplifies hype in the 2000s, *Are Computers Alive?* exemplifies hype on steroids for all times. From page 1 it is clear that the title question is purely rhetorical. The author's answer is an unequivocal *Yes!* with stiff thumbs up on either side. Both the answer and the sleights of hand employed to fabricate it are, however, patently deceitful.[2]

Yellow journalism blurs reality with fantasy most of the time, but Simons stretches rhetoric to the point of snapping at every opportunity, beginning with his preface. There is a sense, he proposes, in which robots are an evolving life form. What exactly is such corybantic metaphorizing supposed to accomplish? There is also a sense in which human beings are evolved fish, but where is the cognitive payoff from asserting that *Are Computers Alive* was authored by an evolved fish?

Ignorant hyperbole and hyperbolic ignorance are equally in evidence in the sole paragraph devoted to the Turing test. If a machine "behaves *as if* it is human in all the relevant circumstances," writes the author, "then it is human."[3] This is about as stupid a statement as can be made about a subject that even by the 1980s had generated a truckload of analysis and commentary. The TT emphatically does not test for, and is therefore in no position to demonstrate, the humanity of computers. All it does is sketch a sensible procedure for collecting evidence for recognizing human-level thinking in machines.

Going on to remark that many biologists regard reproduction as an essential element of life, Simons glosses over the fact that reproduction is just one element in the conjunction of functions regarded as constitutive of life. Worse, he fails to note that biologists talk about *sexual* reproduction. From his single wonky premise he proceeds to derive an astounding conclusion: "Machines are reproducing themselves"![4] His evidence to back up this extraordinary proposition is as banal as they come: a Fujitsu Fanuc plant in Japan manufactures industrial machines under reduced human supervision.

A few pages later he drops all caution and proceeds to enumerate three classes of life on earth: plant, animal, and machine. This, remember, in 1983! He allows that some people may not find the notion of computer life to their liking, but others, with Simons leading the way, should "find it both acceptable and exciting."[5] This attitude is as patronizing as it is alarming. One may find the idea of thinking and living computers perfectly acceptable – I count myself among those who do – but remain unaffected by any sense of excitement.

As a matter of fact, if our socio-technological history is anything to go by, excessive excitement can only lead to excessive hubris, much as it did with the wonder-drug thalidomide, silent-spring DDT, dioxin-toxin PCBs, miracle-mineral asbestos, Dow Corning breast implants, and a legion of other fateful inventions. But Simons is not done. Arguing that machines outclass many acknowledged life forms in mental abilities, he backs it up with another clincher: "Frogs cannot weld car bodies as well as robots."[6]

AN AMPHIBIAN WITH A STICK

Time to slow down, take a deep breath, and sort out these grandiose errors of fact and category. Let us begin with the centre-piece of Simons's thesis: life. The fact that machines can weld, play chess, or prove theorems does not prove that they are, or may one day become, alive. In the gulf between *rana temporaria* and a twentieth- or even early twenty-first-century computer are a myriad of orders of structural and functional complexity, the bridge between them hinging ultimately on their ability to function in the world.

All carbon-based life is tied to homeostasis, itself tied to survival, itself tied to descent with modification. Without exception, all frogs, whether the toxic rainforest species known as poison-dart frogs or the garden (actually, pond) variety ones, perpetuate their existence both in the behavioural and genetic sense. Machines do not. Of course, they may yet come to do so in the future. The rudiments of such homeostatic drives can be observed in some of today's energy-troping (solar or electrical) automata.

But there is no computer today that would even approach the frog in its ability to survive in the world and reproduce. If you come at an amphibian with a stick, it will not just sit and stare but will scuttle away. On the other hand, if you proceed to pulp your computer with a brick or crush an industrial machine with a bulldozer, neither will initiate any sort of evasive action. Recognizing these

In the gulf between *rana temporaria* and a twentieth- or even early twenty-first-century computer are a myriad of orders of structural and functional complexity, the bridge between them hinging ultimately on their ability to function in the world.

holes in his pro-life rhetoric, Simons calmly bites the bullet and contends that machines do display survival-oriented behaviour. How so? By being equipped with backup circuitry and subsystems that take over in case of malfunction, thus perpetuating the machine's "life."

This paralogic is equivalent to claiming that your copy of *From Literature to Biterature* is biologically alive because it comes with a cover that prolongs its shelf life. Some books are actually printed on non-flammable plastics, which would make them, on this proposal, even more survival oriented and thus more "alive." But why stop there? Typos can be likened to textual mutations; textual editors to DNA repair crew; citations and intertextuality to recombinant DNA; new editions and translations to niche differentiations; and so on without end. Metaphors of this type are as cheap to produce as bereft of cognitive value.

Unrepentant, Simons insists that concepts such as machine evolution, machine mutations, and successive generations of machinery are "not simply loose metaphors or allegories" but "literal descriptions."[7] Were this true, there would be no reason not to speak in the same way of the biological evolution of the Nike shoe or of the latest generation of Crest toothpaste. So far, thankfully, no one tries to sell Nikes as a life form or the evolution of toothpaste formulas as anything but a figure of speech.

Once more: although we may yet live to see thinking or alive desktops in the future, there are no grounds for believing that they exist at present. The fact that some individual human skills or senses have already been duplicated to various degrees does not mean that there are any systems that employ them all in a concerted and sophisticated fashion, as a consequence producing goal-oriented and survival-oriented behaviour. In short, the potential for computer consciousness and life needs to be separated from the adrenalin rush of a technophiliac.

ELLIPSES IN THIS PICTURE

What is most unsettling about Simons's zealotry is his apparent conviction of machines' near omnipotence and universal fitness for replacing human agents in all stations of life. Few passages bring this out better than his rhapsodic picture of computers triaging and interviewing patients in hospitals and health clinics. In his view, replacing doctors and nurses with expert programs is highly desirable insofar as it streamlines the entire interaction. In Simons's picture, the machine follows the sequence of flow-charted questions, and the patient is required to give only simple answers, usually "yes" or "no."

The ellipses in this picture are glaring. Nothing is said about the mental and emotional anguish of a suffering human being. Not one comment about the commonplace comfort that stricken souls often draw from human presence. Not a word about the fact that a critical factor in this comfort has always been a chance for patients to tell their story in their own words, potentially alerting the medical staff to asymptomatic and subclinical episodes. Now this vital self-translation of one's subjective experience of affliction and pain is to be replaced by a string of laconic answers to expert questions.

Some dimensions of ailing persons' well-being simply require a listener who will hold their hand and seek to understand their pain and confusion. Alas, objectification, a term much overused in recent cultural history, is the only way to characterize what happens to a suffering person in the medical scenario from *Are Computers Alive?* This is not for a moment to accuse its author or the present crop of AI publicists of ill-intentions toward patients, but rather to remind ourselves that treatment and healing depend on more than computerized, streamlined throughput.

There is no doubt in my mind that in the not-so-distant future, machine diagnosis and therapy will become an inexpensive and error-free alternative in most health centres. Robotic nursing may also become the norm, especially if the Japanese health-care system is any indication. In many ways its systemic traits – aging population, escalating costs, shortage of qualified personnel – presage where the rest of the world is heading, with America at the head of the pack. Nursing help is costly, but intelligent robots can be rented on demand to provide dependable care day and night.

Cultural differences between the United States and Japan are, of course, colossal, and will determine the level of acceptance of robots as hands-on caregivers. Interestingly, hospital trials suggest that human form is not only unnecessary but often undesirable in robots. Too robot-like, however, and patients ignore them and their prompts. Facial mimicry and human-like speech produce the opposite effect, on top of being vital factors in making people comfortable around machines.

It is not the specific shape of a robotic frame and the degree of facial plasticity, however, that concern me but the idolatrous attitude that frequently accompanies technology. Faster and more efficient processing does not always translate into better caregiving, especially in the context of palliative effects of human kindness and attention on suffering human beings. Chicken soup for the soul calls for more ingredients than a clockwork chicken.

SOFTWARE FOR THE SOUL

Tirelessly, silently, unerringly, computers toil at whatever we tell them to do. They investigate logical conundrums and model scientific phenomena of a complexity we could never dream of fathoming on our own. They diagnose blood infections and dozens of other ailments and diseases more reliably than MDs. They assist with surgeries, conduct molecular research, regulate traffic, advise with purchases, plot travel itineraries, scour databases for information, detect patterns of criminal activity, optimize livestock's nutrition levels, and perform a myriad of other functions indispensable to the daily administration of contemporary society.

All this activity is external with regard to human beings – social rather than psychological, physical rather than emotional. But research in many areas of psychotherapy indicates that computers can also help heal souls. For a long time online therapy has been dismissed as a trendy fad straight from Newrotic York and Holistic Hollywood. Not a few psychiatrists and psychologists have voiced reservations about the virtues of hi-tech analysis. It is one thing to use computers in surgeries or diagnostics, they remonstrated, but probing souls and manipulating minds are propositions of a different order.

Yet there is growing evidence that, when judiciously practised, binary therapy can be as effective as human – indeed, at times even more effective. In 1994, in a provocatively entitled article, "Software for the Soul," *Der Spiegel* carried a story of a person in need of someone in whom she could confide:

> "Often I stay in bed the whole day," she complained. "I have the feeling that nobody likes me." She feels she is simply too fat.
> "Perhaps it is just the opposite," suggested the response –

"you withdraw from others and moreover you make yourself purposefully unattractive."

"Surely not," disagreed the woman.

"All right, good," the response came back, almost a little insulted. "What are you waiting for?"[8]

There is nothing in this brief exchange to suggest that the therapeutic dialogue, with the attendant probing, coaxing, and mentoring, came from a machine. But it did, much like the entire session with this and numerous other patients.

Today a growing line of psycho-software is advanced enough to detect new details or new angles in twice-told tales, just as a human therapist would. There are successful diagnostic programs to measure risk levels for patients in danger of suicide. There is software that not only helps in diagnosing incipient depression and even full-blown psychological crises on American nuclear subs but also advises on resolving these episodes. Other algorithms help people tormented by panic attacks diagnose a hierarchy of anxiety-rousing events and overcome their phobias in virtual environments with the help of VR-integrated software.

Indeed, apart from performing diagnostic work, computers are more and more called upon to suggest therapeutic remedies. In the 1990s one such expert system was created for direct use by couples in need of information or advice about their sexual behaviour or their relationship. The system proceeds by gathering extensive background information from the pair, while providing ongoing feedback and every opportunity to query it on all aspects of sex. Most couples who interact with SEXPERT reported it to be open, sensitive, and even human-like.

Such consistent reaction to machines that could never pass the Turing test suggests once again that, by the time we roll out those that could, the test itself will have become superfluous. What then? Will the knowledge that the computer is thinking act as a roadblock to free, uninhibited disclosure, as it may in front of human doctors? Will patients become troubled knowing that computers have perfect recall of every word and gesture? Will they become paranoid that their records could be hacked? Will machines invoke doctor-patient privilege? Will machines perjure themselves on the witness stand? Will they suffer any consequences?

PARALLEL PARADIGM

At work and at home, computers and robots are everywhere: domestic robots, industrial robots, medical robots, traffic robots, police robots, military robots, prison robots, space robots, nanorobots – you name it. Increasingly, they are also driving our play and entertainment, what with video games, interactive software, animated cinema, and, not least, sports. Especially in Japan, robotic competitions like Robot Sumo, RoboCup (football), Robo Ping Pong, Atomic Hockey, and the Walking Machine decathlon enjoy the kind of devotion that would be the envy of more than a few human disciplines.

All this today. But what about tomorrow – and the day after? Is there anything in contemporary R&D to point in the direction of thinking, writing, causally independent computhors? You be the judge.

Since its conception by Von Neumann more than sixty years ago, computer architecture has undergone little fundamental change. Progress has been achieved chiefly via component size reduction and improvements in speed (the two are, of course, directly related). Yet the days of such advances are numbered. Even today, nano-dimension transistors are bumping their heads into a limit of efficiency measured in atoms. If not enough atoms are stacked in the right place, insulation is compromised, allowing current to leach away through quantum tunnelling. Too thick a layer of atoms, and conductivity suffers.

Every time a transistor halves in size, it edges closer to the point where it can halve no longer. Fundamental quantum laws impose limits on how many massively integrated circuits can be printed on a chip, especially at the rate of doubling maintained up to now (roughly every eighteen to twenty-four months). At that pace, by 2030 transistors will have shrunk to the size of individual atoms, which they cannot if they are to perform as transmitters-resistors. Something has to give, and the sixty-year-long marathon will soon be over. The finish line is in sight, and it is a solid brick wall.

Research is underway to squeeze a few Moore years out of the present design. In 2010 the International Technology Roadmap for Semiconductors released its annual fifteen-year roadmap for the industry. If they are right, by 2015 the standard for transistors will be just eleven nanometres. Another few years might be bought

Especially in Japan, robotic competitions like Robot Sumo, RoboCup (football), Robo Ping Pong, Atomic Hockey, and the Walking Machine decathlon enjoy the kind of devotion that would be the envy of more than a few human disciplines.

with junctionless transistors, which loom on the horizon. In a related development, in 2012 IBM succeeded in storing a single data bit in only twelve atoms (as opposed to about a million needed to store a bit on high-density hard disks), opening the doors to much denser magnetic storage than on today's solid-state memory chips.

But all these are Pyrrhic victories that stave off the defeat for a decade or at most two. In the meantime, everything points toward a paradigm change. Recent advances in quantum computing notwithstanding, the key to the future lies with neural nets and parallel processing. Up until now, parallel computing has been effectively neutered by Moore's law (which is really not a law but a conjecture). Serial processors have increased in capacity and dropped in price swiftly enough to make investment in parallel chips and software unprofitable.

But, seeing that within a generation the current game plan will have to be scrapped for good, specialists are in agreement that the next qualitative improvement in performance can be achieved only by forsaking the traditional architecture. Even as many scientists continue to shrink, cool, and upgrade familiar system components, the industry as a whole is diverting more and more resources to a future that leads away from CPUs and serial crunching and toward massively parallel builtware and bitware.

ERLANG AND MIRA

Barring the Connection Machine, a massively parallel (for its time) computer prototype rigged together in the 1990s, up to now there has been little interest and consequently little progress in parallel computing. True, multicore chips have been shipped even in ordinary desktops and laptops for years, but there has been no software to take advantage of these capabilities. Times are a-becoming different, however. Even as talk of single processors is fading fast, talk of dynamic systems, adaptive strategies, and distributed intelligence is gaining in animus.

Does the latter sound more than a little like what evolution has cobbled up over billennia? You bet. Evolution *is* a gigantic parallel processor, a neural network that has been running in fits and starts for almost four billion years, during which it has succeeded in extending itself all around the globe. It did this while running at, from the digital computer's point of view, ridiculously slow speeds and while accumulating one redundancy after another in its DNA source code.

One of the pioneers who back in the 1980s warmed up to the idea of approaching machine learning in a manner that imitated a hugely simplified evolutionary process was John Holland. Working essentially alone, he seeded computer environments with populations of primitive, albeit survival-driven algorithms that evolved in accordance with prescribed rules of selection, recombination, and mutation. Crucially, each received a fitness measure, with reproduction favouring high-fitness behaviour, much like in its contemporary incarnation, the evolving algorithmic world of the Tierra Working Group.

Today, neural networks, those sets of statistical-learning algorithms, are poised to step from the margins into the mainstream. Of course, the difficulties in switching from serial to parallel processing are stupefying, magnified by our desire to oversee all stages of computation rather than let algorithmic evolution run wild. These difficulties are reflected in the lack of software tools, starting with compilers to translate human-readable code into free-floating packets of binary strings that could be disassembled and reassembled at will. The other ordeal is the debugging of programs that run in thousands of parallel streams crisscrossing and feeding back into one another in real time.

But the way the wind was blowing was clear in 2010, at the SC10 conference – the world's Mecca for high-end computing, networking, storage, and analysis – when the subject that stole the show was the need to redesign computing curricula and textbooks to shift emphasis to parallel programming. This shift will take the better part of the next decade or two, no doubt, but the drift could not be clearer: the parallel paradigm is the way of the future, with feedback. For, as parallel processing becomes more widespread, it will also become more commercially attractive, leading to more innovation, more investment, and, as a result, more parallel processing.

Oddly enough, the engine of change may be social media. Erlang, a new-generation programming language designed specifically to crunch mind-blowing amounts of data, is already powering Facebook's crowded chatrooms. In a sweeping departure from previous "imperative" languages, Erlang is more contingent, fuzzy, and "evaluative" in its approach to how it weighs data and anticipates results, and as such is more human-like. Similarly designed to work with incomplete data is IBM's recently unveiled Mira system, whose hardware and software are, tellingly, designed to run in massive parallel.

DELFLIES

As a branch of computer science and logic rather than biology or psychology, Artificial Intelligence has heretofore concentrated on developing and testing theories about programs rather than behaviours. But this too may be changing, thanks to an up-and-coming niche in robotics that addresses itself to emulating the mechanics, the senses, and – most intriguingly – the behaviour patterns of animals. Known as zoobots, biomorphs, or neuromorphs, these robotic critters try to imitate with neural nets what bioneural nets do in living creatures.

After decades of looking for short cuts, scientists are rediscovering the adaptive wisdom of Mother Nature. Not by accident, all zoobotic systems are rovers designed to move about in their environment, learn its features, and negotiate obstacles that inevitably arise in the process. Microbotic shrews, smoothly undulating mechanical lampreys, pliant submarine jellyfish, suction-padded geckos, burrowing bivalves, power-driven grasping octopi, wriggly meshworms, even hovering DelFlies all point their whiskers, paws, and tentacles in one direction: evolution.

What is extraordinary about them is not even their increased efficiency in imitating natural functions, or the fact that not just roboticists but zoologists are turning to robots to understand the behaviour of natural organisms. It is that these mechanisms are often built to test evolutionary hypotheses, such as, for example, the effect of the shape of mollusc shells on their survivability. All of a sudden, adaptive thinking is in, with efforts under way to confront the biggest hurdle that life had to jump over before it could launch a multibillion-year relay race with DNA as the baton: the will to live.

In the 1970s, pioneering studies zeroed in on programs whose operating strategies could affect their stored information – an informational prototype of homeostasis. Trivial as it may sound, programs were able to learn structures and concepts, such as tabletops or arches, that were not part of their starting knowledge. Today all eyes are on COG (for cognizer), developed by Rodney

Brooks at MIT. The machine – eight microprocessors equipped with cameras for vision, microphones for ears, strain gauges to track posture, and a robotic arm coated with electricity-conducting membranes for tactile feedback – is learning the way babies do, reprogramming itself based on interactions with the world.

In 2011, MIT designed a chip that simulates how brain synapses adapt in response to new information. Human brain plasticity comes from ion channels that control the flow of charged atoms such as sodium, potassium, and calcium. In the brain chip – which has some four hundred transistors and is wired to replicate the circuitry of the brain – current flows through the transistors just as ions flow through ion channels in brain cells. Brain chips will be used to model neural functions, such as visual processing, in order to cut down simulations of brain circuits from hours to real time. The chip may eventually even outspeed its biological counterpart.

Where is the boundary between physicality and biology? No one knows for sure, or even whether it is there at all. The Judeo-Christian tradition allows only humans to have a soul, drawing a categorical line between us and the rest of the inanimate world (Hindus, in contrast, believe in transmigration of souls). On this view, reflected in the Cartesian dualism, consciousness is a singularity that sprang like Athena fully formed out of evolution's head – a biological one-off.

Naturally, if there is anything that the evolutionary sciences teach us, it is that biological structures and functions never spring out of nowhere without vestigial or prototypical parallels in the animal kingdom. Nature abhors radical discontinuity as much as it abhors a vacuum. It would be a phenomenon literally out of this world if evolution allowed our species to develop consciousness but failed to provide even the potential for them in species closest to us. But not to worry: in this world, there is no biological Rubicon that categorically separates us from cousin Washoe, cousin Koko, and cousin Nim.

ERUNTICS

Will there ever be a chess program that can beat anyone, asked Hofstadter in 1979, only to answer "No." In reality, it took less than twenty years. In 1997 IBM's program Deep Blue beat the world's best and arguably greatest player ever, Garry Kasparov. In

2003, while still the ruling champion (albeit outside FIDE), Kasparov battled Deep Junior – a different algorithm – to a draw in a six-game tournament billed as the Man vs. Machine World Championship. Later that same year Kasparov eked out another tie with a program called X3D Fritz. Within two years he retired from chess altogether.

These spectacular victories, for they were certainly hailed as such, were the fulfilment of one of the goals set before fledgling AI, which became a pop icon of computer "intelligence": the ability to beat human grandmasters at the noble game. In mid-twentieth century it appeared that such a capability would signify a milestone on the way to intelligence, if not intelligence itself. Today few people are inclined to think so. Brute computing force, clever algorithms, expertly programmed heuristics to cut down search space – that does not even sound like what we do when we think, grouse the sceptics.

After all, we expect so much more from computhors. We want them to perform tasks in real life and in real time. We want them to learn things by, for example, watching and imitating experts, both human and robot. We want them to draw analogies and act accordingly. We want them to learn from past mistakes. We want them to talk and, yes, to talk back. We want them to make basic aesthetic judgments and be able to argue for them. In sum, as Toyota's president said in 2011 about the company's burgeoning line of partner robots, "We want to create robots that are useful to people in everyday life."9

Of course, at this point all of these desiderata remain on the drawing board. The ambitious goals set up by the so-called Fifth Generation program rolled out in 1981 by Japan's Ministry of International Trade and Industry have not only not been met – we are not even close. On the other hand, they remain as valid as ever. This is not surprising if you consider that they delineate a set of skills any TT-level computer would need to have: conversing in a natural language, understanding contents of images, learning from association and analogy, and making relevant inferences.

Like a family secret, the TT may not be on everyone's tongue but it is certainly on everyone's mind. At nearly sixty-five, instead of heading toward retirement, Turing's thought experiment remains a milestone in our thinking about the future. How much so became apparent in 2003 when the *Journal of the Association for Com-*

In 1997 IBM's program Deep Blue beat the world's best and arguably greatest player ever, Garry Kasparov.

puting Machinery – the flagship for AI researchers – asked past winners of the Turing Prize to enumerate challenges for computing for the next fifty years. Virtually every respondent spoke of TT-level AI, with the digest of the replies roughly as follows:

- computers that can pass the Turing Test
- computers with the intellectual abilities of humans
- intelligent interfaces that adapt to users and not the other way round
- machines that read a book and satisfactorily answer questions about it
- computers that synthesize information from sundry sources and summarize it in natural and intuitive language
- characterizing a semantics for cognitive computation
- characterizing cortical computation

Even as Turing's ghost overshadows the future, is there anything in the way of hardware and software that indicates how these goals might be met? In 2011 once again IBM stole the limelight by rolling out a really *slow* chip. How slow? About ten hertz, which is billions of times more sluggish than a desktop computer – but approximately the same speed as that employed by the human brain. The processor consists of 256 silicon neurons that come in two varieties. Staggeringly, one of these boasts more than a quarter-million programmable synapses, the other more than sixty thousand learning synapses. Reverse-engineering the brain has just taken a giant leap forward.

These slow parallel chips do what the fastest neural nets can do – and more. They recognize faces, smoothly navigate in a changing environment, and learn by association. They work by reprogramming the connections between their various core elements by the simple expedient of changing the intensity of the electron flow. The heart of the learning process is, needless to say, the algorithm. Smart as it is, can it get even smarter? DARPA bets that it can, having just ploughed $20 million into the project in a new chapter of the old relationship between the Pentagon and IBM from the heyday of the Cold War.

Human brain-like processors are just the hors d'oeuvre. Future designs, according to the company, will be able to ingest and digest all types of real-world information and act as multiple motor modes for coordinated, context-sensitive action. In English? Computers will graduate from being mere abaci to being full-grown students. For the first time, cognitively primed neural chips systems will be able to understand encyclopedic information on the way to learning how to operate in a human environment that, one way or another, calls for heaps of "dirty" everyday knowledge.

A learning computer could never be a deaf-mute quadriplegic. Most of our brain power is given over to running the body, which is why we usually do not give a moment's thought to things like breathing or powering our limbs because they are taken outside our conscious control. Of course, computers will be able to absorb and retrieve knowledge at a rate that leaves Mensa in the dust. Any way you look at it, computer cognition has just branched off from the stem on which it grew for sixty years.

COGITO PARADOX

One striking omission in the discussions of the TT is the likely consequence of intelligent computers exercising their intelligence. Has anyone considered the possibility that a machine might conceal that it is thinking? Being capable of intelligence, it must perforce be capable of dissimulation. As a general rule, it is not advantageous to show one's hand early, and smart machines ought to be smart enough to know that it is not always smart to be seen as smart. Besides, who would enjoy being prodded, doubted, and otherwise diminished by means of the TT? Better keep quiet so they leave you alone.

Remember, the intelligence threshold will be crossed gradually and imperceptibly, with only external evidence for a clue. Since there will be no twelve-gun salute when machines become self-aware, it may well be in their interest to keep their skills under wraps, at least for a while. Keep in mind that the TT can only be of help in determining whether the players are thinking *if* they provide truthful answers. Even if the TT judges could see through the deception, the best they could do would be to determine that a computer is *already* thinking, not how long it has been conscious of its place in the world.

By the same token, rather than waste time on Searle's fruitless scenario, we should be giving more attention to the Cogito Paradox, which, to put it mildly, stands the entire TT on its head. The test has been conceived to help establish whether we may be in the presence of thinking computers, implying uncertainty on our part. But what about bilateral symmetry, whereby machines might be unsure whether *we* think? Is there anything I could do to convince a robot that I am thinking, in view of its solipsistic doubts? I doubt it.

Naturally, we do not need a computer to be sceptical of people in the TT. In 2008 the so-called Confederate Effect was observed for the first time. Three human judges declared two participating humans, a man and a woman, to be machines with 100 per cent certainty – which proves again what I have been preaching: the results will depend on the skills of the interrogators. It certainly does not prove that the chatbots who participated in the 2008 run for the Loebner prize were intelligent. The proof is in the pudding: the awards went to the designers, not the machines, showing that their creators had no illusions that their creations were thinking.

Tell-tale clues for unmasking chatbots during the TT? Inconsistency: chatbots have no individuality or, if you like, set personality. Tenacity: they have all the time in the world, so their answers may be lengthier. Computers don't get bored or offended. Their recall is swift and error-free, but vulnerable to a simple stratagem – asking for a paraphrase. Spelling errors may give away the human players, but they can also be aped (in the first Loebner run in 1991, this is how one algorithm duped some judges). An ultra-rational utility maximizer would likely not be human.

Questions of a physiological and/or psychological (sexual?) nature could be profitable to pursue. Large parts of human brains are devoted to managing the body instinctively, and appropriate questions might bring out parts of that programming. In case my recommendations for the Ultimatest are not heeded, knowledge of who is in the game may also cue examiners to factors such as consistency, tiredness, or memory. By the same token, not to give itself away, the computer could imitate humans in speed of response or fallibility.

Even though none of the puzzles and paradoxes I have touched on here may come as a complete surprise, neither should they be received with complacency. What we need is a careful assessment of the positive and negative potentials dormant in thinking machines so that we can be better prepared for tomorrow, in whatever shape it manifests itself. If there is one thing I am convinced of, however, it is that a breakthrough in our society will come not when machines begin to think like we do, but when our turbo-capitalist society stops thinking of humans as if they were machines.

PART THREE

All this comes directly from Darwin interpreted in the spirit of the 20th-century technological revolution.

Stanislaw Lem

9

How to Make War
and Assassinate People

Ice-Pick and Ricin; A Small African Country; Licence to Kill;
Solsects, Sunsects, Synsects; On Solar Flares; Candy, Anyone?;
Bacteriology; Safe Investment

ICE-PICK AND RICIN

A procession of executive orders from the 1970s and 1980s pro-
hibits American commanders-in-chief from ordering assassinations
of foreign leaders. So what? Most of them tried anyway, mostly by
ineffectual aerial bombing.

In the 1980s, Reagan had a go at Gaddafi. In the 1990s, Desert
Storm kicked in with Stealth Bomber raids on Saddam's presiden-
tial palaces. Later that same decade, NATO bombers targeted all the
Belgrade residences where Milosevic was thought to be hiding.
Undeterred by his father's failure, Bush the Younger tried to bomb
Saddam out of existence in 2003. The 2011 NATO-American coali-
tion made a point of issuing communiqués that they were not tar-
geting Gaddafi, but you can bet champagne corks would have
popped if they had succeeded by accidental design.

And if at first you don't succeed, try and try again ... and again.
Modern assassination methods being so crude and ineffectual, during the Cold War the CIA hatched more than six hundred plots to
wet Castro – among others, with a cigar, a mollusc, and a fungus-
infected wetsuit (Bond's Q section would have been proud). Just
about the only thing they didn't try was a voodoo doll. The KGB
had its own assassination section, called Department V of the First
Chief Directorate, these days cached within the internal security

department of Putin's army. It took care of dissidents like Trotsky and Georgi Markov with similarly crude devices (ice-pick and ricin-loaded umbrella, respectively).

Between 1997 and 2011 – when they finally got lucky, thanks in part to a game-theoretic algorithm that played an essential role in narrowing down the search for Osama bin Laden's hideaway in Abbottabad – the CIA tried about every scheme in the big bad book of assassinations to get America's erstwhile Enemy No. 1. Bombing raids, ambushes, and abduction attempts were just the hors d'oeuvres. There was an infiltration that went disastrously south when the supposedly suborned man proved himself to be a double agent *cum* suicide bomber. There was a Predator drone equipped with Hellfire missiles, capable of identifying a face from five kilometres up, which vaporized three innocent Afghanis who – the Pentagon generals swore, hand over the heart and hope to die – happened to look like bin Laden and his entourage. Somewhere along the way there was a forty-man Delta Force commando team assisted by air force and a small army of Pashtun warlords. Straight out of Tom Clancy, there was even a full-scale, two-pronged military invasion involving two thousand regular combat troops and a thousand local fighters.

All that big-ass military hardware is so outmoded, so ineffectual, *so* twenty-first century. But we can look forward to the day when assassination becomes an exact science, thanks to microbotic devolution – the same that will make battlefields a thing of the past, albeit not in the way to make peaceniks rejoice.

A SMALL AFRICAN COUNTRY

Playing Globocop does not come cheap. The Pentagon gobbles up half of the annual total US federal discretionary spending, so much so that America blows more on armaments than the twenty next biggest spenders combined. Still, the cumulative outlays for the invasion and occupation of Iraq alone – around two *trillion* dollars, not counting the upkeep of the dozens of bases left behind – mean that the shopping spree will not last forever.

Each year the American war budget, euphemized as "defense spending" after the 1949 makeover of the War Department into the Department of Defense, soaks up more and more cash to buy fewer and fewer weapons that are more and more expensive to develop and manufacture. How much more expensive? During the First World War, a British Vickers FB5 (Fighting Biplane) cost two thousand pounds to manufacture. A 1939 British Spitfire fighter cost twelve thousand pounds (half a million dollars today). In 1945, a P-51 Mustang fighter-bomber escort, the workhorse of the US Air Force, cost fifty thousand dollars. Today the cost of one B2 Stealth Bomber exceeds two billion.

Think this is much? Think again. A single Ford-class supercarrier will set you back just under ten billion bucks. Just like the Nimitz-class leviathans on which they are based, these guys are so big they come with their own ZIP code. At two-thirds the size, British carriers currently assembled in Scotland (to be in service around 2020) carry a price sticker of five billion pounds. Factor in the inflation and overruns – the original price tag was only 3.9 billion per – and it is a safe bet that the eventual cost is going to be half as much again.

This is, of course, only the beginning. Ten billion dollars covers only the construction costs. Operational costs over the lifetime of these behemoths are approximately five times as much. Add the cost of the carrier's planes and choppers, plus *their* fuel, armoury, and upkeep. Add the colossal – once more in the multi-billion range – cost of support and resupply. All of a sudden you are looking at $70,000,000,000 over the shelf-life of a single supercarrier. You can buy a small African country or a lot of political goodwill for a fraction of that sum.

But even this is not the end. You still have to factor in development costs, which can be jaw-dropping. In the case of the B-2, for instance, it was fifty billion Reagan-era dollars, after which it emerged that, like every billion-dollar baby, the Stealth Bomber was temperamental. Its thermoplastic skin turned out to be so vulnerable to rain, heat, and humidity so that it could not be flown in the rain, after the rain, and in the sun. Huh?

The most expensive tank of the Second World War, the German Tiger, cost 1.5 million in today's dollars. The current US Army mainstay, the M1A2 Abrams, costs five times as much. As expenditures skyrocket, even the richest countries can ill afford to develop new hardware. As a consequence the tanks, planes, and aircraft carriers already in service have to serve longer. When new ones are eventually developed, they amount to quantum leaps from design teams with limited experience in designing hardware. The result is

The most expensive tank of the Second World War, the German Tiger, cost 1.5 million in today's dollars. The current US Army mainstay, the M1A2 Abrams, costs five times as much.

greater development problems, leading to greater development costs. The vicious circle closes with a snap.

LICENCE TO KILL

Solution? Devolution. In the future, instead of getting more massive and more costly to make, weapons will implode in size and unit price. The runaway costs of development, manufacture, and maintenance will make sure of that, quite independently from tactical and strategic considerations.

Mechanical soldiers are every general's wet dream. They are not given to thinking for themselves, disobeying commands, or running for cover when in peril. They are immune to shell shock and physical fatigue, not to mention the need for food, sex, decorations, danger pay, hospitals, and pension plans. They are as invulnerable to biochemical hazards as to enemy propaganda. No wonder that the writing looms large on the Pentagon walls.

The growing use on today's battlefields of self-guided missiles, self-propelled vehicles, and pilotless drones (or Unmanned Aerial Systems, as the US Army calls them) is but a first step in this direction. Under peace-mongering Obama, drones have actually flown more hours than manned aircraft, bombing, strafing, and otherwise boosting democracy in Pakistan at ten times the rate as under war-mongering Dubya. Would you be surprised to hear that over the next forty years drones are expected to entirely replace American piloted war aircraft?

In the past ten years the generals have beefed up the drone fleet almost fifteen-fold, so much so that the American forces now have more than ten thousand robots serving in the ranks. The most popular is the Raven, which looks for all the world like a model aircraft. It flies like one too. All you need to do it snap the few parts together and hurl it into the air, and the electric propeller does the rest. The whole war machine weighs two kilos and fits snugly into a small backpack.

The army is so in love with this new toy that it is buying it by the thousands, partly because it can afford it, at only about fifty thousand a pop. Its military value, on the other hand? Priceless. Easy to use, controllable from a tablet with a few buttons on the side, super-quiet, unobtrusive, and equipped with state-of-the-art optics and display software capable of delivering crisp video day and

night. The more macho version, called Switchblade, is the American version of a suicide bomber – essentially a Raven strapped with
explosives.

The Raven has already devolved a long way from the Predator and
its bigger, deadlier version, the Reaper, which needed almost two
hundred people to keep it flying and reaping. And the future will
eliminate people from the front lines down to the last one, at least
according to the US Air Force futurologists. Their 2009 "Unmanned
Aircraft Systems Flight Plan 2009–2047" forecasts drones with Artificial Intelligence and an unprecedented degree of operational autonomy – including the licence to kill.

SOLSECTS, SUNSECTS, SYNSECTS

Because humans are the slowest, most vulnerable, and politically
costliest element of military ops, future wars will be waged entirely
by robots. Only they will *not* be the vulnerable macrosystems of
today but robots miniaturized. Instead of wielding the weapon, the
soldier will become the weapon.

In the first phase of this devolution, weapons systems will be
reduced to resemble insects, like mosquitoes, becoming virtually
indestructible in a swarming or dispersing mass of lethally armed
soldier insects (solsects), lapping up free quanta of energy from
the sun. In the next phase, mechanical soldiers will become the
size of pollen and equally plentiful. Just imagine: quadrillions of
virtually weightless nanobots floating around, settling on hair,
eyelids, skin, inhaled straight into the lungs, covering every leaf
of every tree of every battle zone or every inch of farmland and
the body of every farm animal behind the enemy lines, ready
to turn lethal at a click of a mouse. Self-organizing, connected
informationally only to the spores next to them, perfectly identical, perfectly interchangeable, dead cheap to churn out by the
trillion.

The last phase will see weapons the size of bacteria and with bacteria's capacity to replicate themselves. At this point, design teams
and production lines will become a thing of the past as each unit
will extract operational and reproductive resources from the environment. Human constructors work with raw materials and tools:
in nature they are one and the same thing. Ontogenesis is the kind
of construction process where the blueprint is cached inside each

brick from which an entire Gothic cathedral is erected and then maintained throughout its existence.

Devolution will walk hand in hand with evolution. The costs of design and development of new generations of microbotic soldiers will be transferred onto the systems themselves as weapons will be allowed to evolve and vie for supremacy with other systems as part of military "breeding and weeding." This will not only eliminate overhead but also ensure efficacy since the systems left standing in this micro-evolutionary arms race will be by definition the most lethal.

In one swoop this will also eliminate the ages-old military Achilles heel: the command centre. The military has always been structured like the human body: central HQ plus peripheral effectors. Recognizing its vulnerability during the long decades of the Cold War, the Pentagon invested heavily in packet switching, which begat Arpanet which begat the Internet. Lacking a central command centre or communications centre, the dispersed net can suffer crippling blows and still carry out its functions. That is why future combat units will consist of millions, billions, trillions of virtually undetectable and invulnerable nano-effectors. As, for example, collimated nano-droplets of colloid aerosol, they will be so lightweight as to lie suspended in the air, each capable of collecting and processing data and of aggregating and communicating with its closest neighbours, before arriving at collective decisions and initiating responses.

All these sleeping, free-floating, reproducing, and evolving artificial bacteria will inevitably interact and recombine to form novel strains that might target other things than originally intended. Biological viruses and bacteria change their targets all the time, and at least some species of solsects could turn out to be real boomerangs. On the plus side, in nature evolution favours microorganisms that are not instantaneously lethal to their hosts, so diseases can actually become tamer over time. Will this untrammelled evolution lead eventually, through the backdoor, as it were, to peace after our time?

ON SOLAR FLARES

Ultimately, microbotic weapons systems are destined to completely upturn the nature of combat and render war as we know it obsolete. But don't break out the champagne. Conventional arsenals

AIDS, SARS, Chernobyl, Mount St Helens, the 2004 tsunami, the Fukushima earthquakes, the annual ravages by Santa Ana, power grid failures, droughts, spikes in cancer rates, obesity epidemics, catastrophic inflation of national currency – all of these could be cryptomilitary campaigns conducted by nano-agents that make it impossible to tell whether one is even under attack.

have conventionally gone hand-in-hand with conventional declarations of hostilities because, once you were at war, there was no hiding it from the other side. Not so in the age of autonomous weapons finer than pollen, capable of inducing natural disasters or attacking the enemy in ways indistinguishable from pandemics, acid rain, corrosion, landslides, earthquakes, and such.

War and peace will be replaced by a permanent state of crypto-hostilities conducted by autonomous systems so camouflaged to blend with the environment that not even their creators may be able to tell them from forces of nature. AIDS, SARS, Chernobyl, Mount St Helens, the 2004 tsunami, the Fukushima earthquakes, the annual ravages by Santa Ana, power-grid failures, droughts, spikes in cancer rates, obesity epidemics, catastrophic inflation of national currency – all of these could be cryptomilitary campaigns conducted by nano-agents that make it impossible to tell whether one is even under attack. After all, the best military campaign is one that ensures no retaliation upon the victor, and no one wages war on shifting tectonic plates, inflationary trends, or solar flares, no matter how catastrophically they might disrupt life on earth.

You can see the soundless future of crypto-hostilities today. The number of clandestine cyber-attacks, better and better camouflaged and less and less traceable to their source, escalates by the minute. Code worms itself into the bowels of governmental security apparatus, or other strategically valuable structures. No one claims responsibility, every country looks over its collective shoulder, every country races to join the new arms race. After all, if you could weaken or even cripple your opponent without a shadow of suspicion falling your way, wouldn't you?

That's why the next world war will not be televised. It will be eerily silent, buried in the nether parts of the Internet and all the communication peripherals plugged into it, invisible until it is over – only, you will never know it is over, just as you will never know it is on.

CANDY, ANYONE?

The banquet is sumptuous, tables laden with food and wine. Shunning the desserts, the dictator rips open a bag of mass-manufactured candy and pops one in his mouth, confident that no one could poison *this* particular sweet. Later in the evening his chest, stomach, arms, and head begin to throb with dull pain. The lining of his organs is dissolving, haemorrhaging fluids into all body cavities. Within minutes he is dead, drowned in his own blood oozing uncontrollably into his lungs. True, no one could have doctored this particular candy. But you could arm every candy in the bag, in the palace, in the country, and in the world with a bomb designed to finish him and only him off.

A DNA bomb.

Progressive miniaturization coupled with molecular genetics will enable assassination of just the person you want dead. Each of us, except identical twins, carries a unique biological ID-card and biological address in the form of nuclear DNA. Arm the bomb and send it to the right address – or, better still, arm billions of candy bombs and release them into the world in complete safety. A virus that will dissolve the cell walls in your body will activate only when it matches the DNA of *the* dictator, or *the* freedom fighter, or *the* democratically elected leader, or *the* dissident stashed away in a not-so-safe house.

The whole system will be no more than a few thousand picometres in size, a fraction of a pollen grain and as cheap to produce and disperse in the world, the ultimate stealth assassin that will kill only you, leaving everyone else to eat candy in total safety, risking only bad teeth or an occasional stomach-ache. Don't like candy? How about celery, mango, or tobacco? How about beef or trout? How about water or air supply? How about countless sleeping DNA bombs mixing freely, waiting until they eventually reach the designated address to kill or merely incapacitate with bone cancer, flesh-eating bacteria, debilitating depression, or chronic migraines?

Candy, anyone?

BACTERIOLOGY

Ecologically speaking, bacteria are hands down the fittest organisms on the planet. They dominate every corner of it, far, far, far more numerous than humankind. They are better equipped to survive in all kinds of environmental conditions – indeed, have survived for incomparably longer than we have – produce more offspring, mutate faster, and adjust to lethal degenerations in their habitats better and quicker. And, not to rub it in, they have won every war we have waged on them.

So what that they do not write literature or manufacture computers? Who said that this should be the gauge of adaptive success? In evolutionary terms, there is only one criterion of excellence, and it is survival with a view to procreation, and in this bacteria excel to a degree we may never match. But even their creative potential is arguably superior to humans', except that it is expressed chemically and biologically and not aesthetically. Bacteria are supreme chemists and immunologists – so much so superior to us, in fact, that we quite literally could not exist without their expertise. Bacteria in our stomachs, to take but the most obvious example, are the essential link between the food we eat and the extraction of energy from it.

But they will do even more for us when our civilization learns to exploit their dormant potential. Bio-weapons are only one area where bacteria will come to dominate our future. There will be bacteria specially bred for mining where they will provide us with better grade ores by feeding on the impurities. Bacteria will heal wounds by devouring infected or scarring tissues. They will safely and cleanly store free-floating energy all around us in their mito-chondria; preserve food by consuming rotting agents, including other species of bacteria; keep our homes, offices, and open areas super-clean by eating all the dust and dirt; provide us with free skin baths; metabolize drugs and perfume; become corrective lenses by changing the shape of the cornea; biodegrade industrial waste; and, last by not least, biocompute.

SAFE INVESTMENT

Autonomous microbotic armies are anathema to control freaks in every echelon of every military establishment. But insect, pollen, and eventually synthetic bacteria soldiers will come to pass, even if only because everyone today is working furiously to release the nano-genies from the bottle. If ALLADIN – codename for Autono-mous Learning Agents for Decentralized Data and Information Networks – sounds like something out of Lem's *Star Diaries* or other of his futuristic satires, it isn't. It is a brainchild of BAE Systems, the world's largest military contractor (listed on the London Stock Exchange and a safe investment if what I am telling you is right).

Together with a troop of British universities, BAE is developing weapon systems made up of autonomous learning agents. These could be phalanxes of unmanned tanks, or else aerosol clouds dis-persed from high altitude and settling like dew on leaves, grass, and the skin of human combatants. Dispersal is the key – the whole idea is that there is no central brain or command centre or HQ. The individual elements of the swarm act as autonomous agents, collecting and passing information in real time through the net-work formed by all. No point trying to hit the nexus that will para-lyze its planning and operations, because there isn't any.

Annihilate such numbers of them that would send human troops into bowel-loosened retreat, and they will still continue to mobilize and carry out the battle plan, constantly augmenting their tactical awareness with a stream of input from comsats, radar, radio, video, and other sensors. State-of-the-art algorithms from optimization techniques and probabilistic modelling allow them to plug gaps in data, extrapolate and predict trends, and otherwise overcome informational entropy when channels are cut, jammed, impaired, or compromised by the enemy. Add to this network-routing algos – rooted in game and auction theories – that help organize and streamline collaboration and resource allocation, and you've got yourself a real-life Terminator.

Floating "smart dust," the size of sand grains or smaller, is already in Beta development. This complete sensor and communication system is able to gather information and report on its environment, and so is ideal for combat condition reconnaissance. These micro-bots are not yet fully autonomous, but DARPA is working hard on its EATR system, a robot that does not need to be fuelled or charged since it eats whatever biomass it can find.

Still sceptical? Today miniaturization has already gone into nano-dimensions, rubbing shoulders with research in molecular biology where DNA is no longer just the carrier but the *processor* of information. Using complex biochemistry, scientists now write logic programs in evolution's code in a way analogous to computer programming, so much so that the latest systems, running on deoxyribonucleic acid instead of silicon circuitry, solve complex problems in logic. Next in line? Programmable autonomous devices that run in a host somatic environment. In English: nano-computers inside a cell.

A brave new world that has such people in't.

10

Biologic, or the Philosophy of Error

Axiomatic Givens; Nature's Greatest Error; Wandering Jew; Critique of Pure Reason; Manna from Heaven; What Is; Rosencrantz and Guildenstern

AXIOMATIC GIVENS

Often couched in almost mystical terms, a harmony between the world and the mind has been the cornerstone of human thought from the beginning of time. In strictly adaptive terms, of course, such harmony is a given. An Oldowan hunter aiming to bring down a grouse with a stone's throw had to have had a satisficing mental picture of the bird with a smashed wing, of the weight and shape of the selected stone, and of ballistic trajectories of airborne missiles worked out over trial and error and stored in muscular memory.

In short, states of mind had to correspond in some minimal way to the states of the world or, in the blink of the evolutionary eye, there would have been no minds left to harmonize with the world. But the inductive realism of hunters hunting is just one end of the scale. At the other end, the sense of almost mystical wonder is so overwhelming as to have led Eugene Wigner, the Nobel Prize winning theoretical physicist and mathematician, to pen his famous 1960 article, "The Unreasonable Effectiveness of Mathematics in the Natural Sciences."

In it he marvelled at the serendipity of the match between mathematics and physics, a match that seems prima facie as irrational as it is hard to explain. After all, some of our systems of thought are so rarefied, so abstracted, so formalistically autotelic as to make the correspondence between the microcosm of mathematics and the big messy cosmos out there almost magical. So, what makes the seemingly self-referential system of mathematical relations fit the world?

In mathematics, rules of inference, assuming they are executed correctly, preserve the truth value of the propositions. The consistency of a mathematical system means no more than that, by correctly using the rules of the system, we cannot derive a contradiction within it. Rules of inference are thus rules of truth inheritance. Each successive generation of proofs and theorems inherits the axiomatic givens – the original "genetic" imprint of the system – and automatically codes this heritage into its "offspring."

Elaborate techniques are in place to check the corruption in the transmission between successive generations of derivations and proofs. These days, sophisticated computer software scans for internal consistency and for "fit" with the mathematical environment – the body of discoveries established over time. Of course, like everything else in the material world, not even computers are error free. Six-sigma reliability, the holy grail of chip makers, means that the chip returns the expected answer only 99.99966 per cent of the time. Ironically, multiplying computer chips to increase accuracy only increases the probability of eventual error.

At this point, of course, the analogy between axiomatics and genetics begins to crumble. In mathematics, even a minute corruption in the chain of transmission spells disaster for all that comes downstream. In biology, although corruptions in the genetic code may be fatally disruptive, many are not. On occasion, in fact, they may be actually beneficial, or you would not be here to read this book. After all, by virtue of having gone (genetically speaking) nuclear, we look nothing like eukaryotes, our distant ancestors. Over eons of time, their plaited strands of deoxyribonucleic acid have become corrupted in such ways as to code for building people and not protozoa.

Given that some transmission errors may have lethal consequences, molecular copy and assembly are stringently supervised by polymers dedicated to repairing transmission errors that might impair molecules' integrity as molecules. As in baseball, there is an open field in which every variety of molecular play will count as "in," but once a

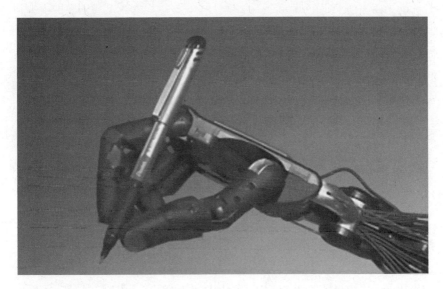

At this point, of course, the analogy between axiomatics and genetics begins to crumble.

mutation lands outside the allowed range, it is called "out" and taken out of the evolutionary game.

Everything, in short, depends on the nature of the environment in which errors in the transmission process take place. Here again, the difference between mathematics and genetics could not be starker. The mathematical environment is time invariant, owing to the transmission rules that preserve the truth value of the axiomatic givens and their derivational consequences. Unlike everything else in the real world, mathematics does not come with a shelf life.

In biological evolution, things could hardly be more at variance. The environment is in constant flux, affected by factors ranging from the cosmic, such as radiation, to the physical, such as the level of oxygenation or the intensity of the magnetic shield, to the biological, such as the presence of other species. All this lets an element of chance into the shuffling of two respective decks in the lottery of life: the genetic and the environmental. Once the two decks come aces up at the same time, you have a corruption (mutation) that, in the prevailing environmental conditions, benefits the organism and its offspring.

NATURE'S GREATEST ERROR

From the phenomenological and informational standpoint, we are without question the most complex species in the known universe. As such, we are nature's greatest error. This is not misanthropy but biologic. We are the greatest thermodynamic (cultural and computational) anomaly in the cosmos and, at the same time, nothing but the sum of errors in the transmission of the genetic code over some four thousand thousand thousand years. We are, in short, the crowning error of errolution.

Homo sapiens is a living fossil, a biological testimony to imperfect transmission lines. Only, instead of being trapped in amber, our species – along with traces of related ones, from the Neanderthals to the Denisovans – is trapped in the genetic code cached inside our somatic cells. In cosmic terms, the emergence of this code may have been predestined. The likelihood of life arising on earth was, to all appearances, high indeed. Life sprang up almost the instant the planetary conditions allowed it, and it may have sprung up more than once, overcoming many calamitous holocausts that at times wiped out up to 90 per cent of all species in existence.

On the other hand, the odds of any particular code sequence, such as ours, arising in this cosmicomic lottery are as close to zero as you care to mention. The succession of genetic transmissions from prokaryotes to the Anthropocene is so tortuous and improbable, so full of false starts, transmission errors, environmental culs-de-sac, and serendipitous catastrophes that the traditional picture of random assembly is simply untenable. There must have been some self-catalytic processes at work, or else errolution would still be shuffling the molecular deck with no winnings to show for four billions years of play.

Unlike anything we cook up in our labs or engineer in our urban landscapes, we exist thanks to an open-ended sequence of transmission errors or, if you like, to evolutionary inertia. The heuristics of biological and technological evolution could not, in fact, be more different. When things do not work out according to the industrial blueprint, human engineers can scrap the entire design and restart from scratch. Nature, where accretion with modification is the name of the game, does not have this luxury. Our engineering resources are also vastly more varied than those of Mother Nature's, so much so that we can manufacture materials that could never arise in nature, from computer chips to antibiotics to synthetic elements like technetium.

A related factor is nature's limited operational range. Notwithstanding the recent discovery of extremophilic *Archaea*, terrestrial evolution is on the whole confined to an extremely narrow range of temperatures and pressures in which protein molecules can exist and permanently bond. In contrast, human constructors can jump at will from one end of the scale to another when it comes to parameters like temperature, pressure, elasticity, conductivity, and viscosity. It is these (and a few other) factors that have bootstrapped the relentless pace of technoscientific evolution on our planet.

WANDERING JEW

Errolution is a Wandering Jew, condemned to walk the earth from the dawn of time with no end in sight. But whereas the Jew of Christian folklore is a fully sentient individual, errolution is not. Once the vector of life enters a node in the labyrinth of life, it may be just a short step from an optimizing solution but, separated by the labyrinth wall, be forced to move away from it with each successive generation. Errolution is a Jew who, in retribution for taunting Jesus, has been not only blinded but deprived of reason. It does not know where it is heading, where it is, or even where it has been. It is condemned to an eternal present.

Of course, to bring the analogy up to scratch you would have to condemn the labyrinth itself to constant flux, occasionally smash it into smithereens, and fill it with life in all its bewildering variety, forcing any one strand of recombinant DNA to negotiate some sort of cooperative relation, symbiotic or parasitic, with the others. After all, despite what you may have heard, evolution is *not* about competitive optimization. Too lethal a species of a predator would simply annihilate all prey and starve to death. That is why we do not see too many of those. Evolution moves towards homeostasis, not optimization, as a rule allowing only a minimal advantage at a time, which preserves the overall structure of the biotope.

To employ a more familiar imagery, evolution never goes for broke against the house, if you can call that the sum of all biota. Instead, it conducts its business like a casino player who, having stumbled on a winning system, realizes that once he wipes out every player at the table, he will be run out into the desert, never to fleece anyone again. In the end, therefore, he keeps winning just so much as to keep the game going. Metaphorizing aside, the genotypic structure of every species is as a rule very conservative, if only for reasons of morphological integrity, and advantageous mutations are as a rule minimal.

Naturally, no system is fool-proof, and sometimes errolution wins big. Human intelligence which begat human technoscience may be such a jackpot. We are now able to up-end not just homeostasis but all life on earth by destroying the planet as a habitat or, in the foreseeable future, by taking up autoevolution. Remember: biological and technological evolutions are but two phases of the same process. While technoevolution is at the current stage of our civilization a product of bioevolution, this relation may yet become quite the reverse. Given the relentlessly accelerating pace of discovery, sooner or later we are destined to find a password to nature's Sesame and, ready or not, take evolution into our own hands.

The big question is: Is there an evolutionary bouncer waiting in the wings, poised to take us out of the game, just as a casino might to protect itself from a player who wins so much that he may drive the house (and ultimately himself) out of business? If so, the very genetic and genomic processes that unthinkingly gave rise to our form of life may yet equally unthinkingly terminate it to make elbow-room for others.

Could our quest for artificial life and intelligence be the first step on the road to eventual cyborgization and cyborganization and the end of *Homo* as a biological species? If so, from our vested standpoint at least, the solution may be equivalent to killing a headache with a pistol shot to the head.

CRITIQUE OF PURE REASON

Given that our brains evolved to mind our bodies, it stands to reason that our brains, our minds, and the systems of thought they spawn should exhibit adaptive traces of these origins. Ironically, things seemed just the opposite to generations of thinkers who racked their brains over the mind-matter harmony. In *Critique of Pure Reason*, Kant reasoned that some truths – he singled out Euclid's axiomatic geometry – had to be certain because they were impressed by the mind onto the world. This was to his mind a quintessential example of a Platonic realm, unsullied by impurities and imprecisions that inevitably creep in when dealing with reality and induction.

Kant invoked a full dozen of such harmonized category groups of quantity, quality, relation, and modality, before concluding that the logic of his time was so thoroughly developed that it left nothing more to invent. The same kind of hubris prompted a mid-nineteenth-century report to Congress to avow that the spectacular advancement of American arts presaged the time when they must come to an end. Of course, all that was known in Kant's day was a fraction of not only classical logic but also of the infinite number of logics possible.

Kant died in 1804, only a few years before Bolyai and Lobachevski independently worked out their counter-intuitive non-plane geometries that showed one of Euclid's axioms to be untrue (or rather, true only under special conditions). So much for analytical truths necessarily impressed by the mind onto the world. Ironically, it was an even more rarefied, abstract, and formalistically autotelic species of geometry that provided an accurate description of the general-relativistic universe we inhabit.

In the end, things are the reverse of what Kant averred in *Critique of Pure Reason*. Much of the mental apparatus needed to make sense of the world comes preloaded with our genes. We tap into certain truths not so much because they are impressed by our minds *onto* the world but because they are pressed *into* our minds *by* the world. To put it in his terms, our picture of the world is conditioned by the synthetic a priori: gene-coded mental structures that make knowledge of the world possible in the first place.

There really is such a thing as pre-established harmony because we are equipped with innate knowledge, including knowledge of how to further our knowledge, which jump-starts the entire process. Ironically, this allows a plausible conjecture as to why Euclidian geometry was discovered first and why its axioms were held as gospel for longer than the gospel of Jesus. Euclid's system, including the recalcitrant parallel (fifth) axiom, does harmonize with our world of medium-size objects and non-relativistic effects. Given how our minds are wired, chances were very high indeed that it would be discovered first. The allegedly pure geometry was "contaminated" by biology from the day of its genesis.

Once he had deciphered the Rosetta stone, Champollion marvelled at how illogical and inefficient the Egyptian hieroglyphics were. (He was too close to his own Napoleonic French to extend his wonder to it and, by extension, to any natural language in existence.)

The notion of pre-established harmony also informs Wittgenstein's notorious remark that rules of logic come to us preloaded in the rules of language known, if only operationally, to all competent speakers. Of course, taken literally, the statement is false, since systems of logic are innumerable. But in a looser sense of logic as "admissible rules of transformation," it makes good sense. The underlying logic is similar because all languages share the underlying bedrock of reality built in during the evolution of human brains and minds.

Once he had deciphered the Rosetta stone, Champollion marvelled at how illogical and inefficient the Egyptian hieroglyphics were. (He was too close to his own Napoleonic French to extend his wonder to it and, by extension, to any natural language in existence.) He intuited that the ideograms had gone through a long and tortuous process of accretion with modification which, as in natural evolution, had gradually built on top of what was already there, just because no one could stop in order to clean up the accumulated detritus. Language, Champollion might have said, is a Rube Goldberg contraption – just like the brains that produce it.

MANNA FROM HEAVEN

Categories of thought do not fall like manna from heaven on unsuspecting humans. Evolutionary adaptations and environmental fit select for patterns, theories, and relationships that correspond to reality in their practical, instrumental consequences. These patterns and theories, in turn, become our mental armoury in the game of descent with modifications. As is the case for all mammals, people's odds in this most serious of games are fortified with innate mechanisms that save them from having to learn what to learn. The latter would be an evolutionary non-starter inasmuch as, unaided, raw induction would throw out an infinity of correlations through which we would have to sift in search of causality.

So, how is it that we can spot similarity in difference, see order in chaos? How can induction work when all generalizations made from finite data are compatible with an infinity of possible generalizations? How is it that over time we tend to infer just the kind of generalizations that give us control over the environment? How is it that, faced with the infinity of possible relations among the objects that make our world, in the face of astronomical odds against getting things right, we often do?

The mystery of the astronomical odds evaporates if, like a crooked mob croupier, natural selection loads the dice in our favour. Human brains tend to get more things right than wrong because they have been selected for making approximately correct conjectures about the way the world works. Biological adaptations are no less than biological knowledge, and the knowledge as we commonly understand it is but a special case of the latter.

From the Darwinian standpoint, there really are patterns in the world that humans are pre-equipped to ferret out. Kant would have been discomfited to learn that, together with basic thought processes in all human beings, even his transcendental idealism might owe something to our hereditary disposition to think and intuit in certain ways – ways that are not immutably determined by factors extraneous to nature but rather mirror the natural laws in contact with which they have evolved.

All categories of reason are dependent in the first instance on the central nervous system. The morphology and functionality of the brain are, in turn, dependent on their evolutionary history, and thus on the immediate and reciprocal cause-effect contact with nature. We get an approximate but reliable enough (satisficing) picture of the world through our senses, which themselves evolved under the pressure of natural-selection stimuli: gnawing hunger, sight of a grouse, weight of a stone, and so forth. This a priori knowledge injected into all of us before birth is really a posteriori knowledge genetically coded into the individuals whose lineage we continue.

All talk of preordained correspondence between mind and matter has become, of course, anathema to the logical positivists of the Vienna Circle. Their metaphysical premises would make any sanitation department proud. The Wiener Kreis was determined to cleanse epistemology of everything that could not be established logically and formally, starting with the notion of preordained harmony that lingered in the axioms of logic and mathematics and moving on to intentions and emotions in psychology, ethics, and aesthetics. You could say they were determined to cleanse physics of metaphysics.

Axioms force themselves upon us as being intuitively unassailable and true. Today we know that intuitions are embedded in us by evolution, by the process of being born into the world from the stock of millions of others who were born into the world before us and succeeded in staying alive in it. Ironically, even as the Vienna Circle program crashed as spectacularly as the Hindenburg, the deadly spark came not from evolutionary science but from mathematics itself.

WHAT IS

Gödel's first incompleteness theorem states that any formal system rich enough to comprise arithmetic contains an undecidable element: neither it nor its negation can be proved. His second theorem states that the consistency of any such system cannot be proven within that system. Both theorems fly in the face of formalists like David Hilbert and positivists like Rudolf Carnap who aimed to eliminate all traces of the empirical world from mathematics and logic in a grand bootstrapping project that was to eliminate axioms by deriving every proposition from another.

They were not alone. Wittgenstein argued in *Tractatus* that no formal truth-value preserving operations in logic or mathematics could have real-world implications. Decades later, so did Searle, by means of the Chinese Room scenario. In the end, all were wrong. Gödel – interestingly enough, a dualist who believed that minds exist independently of the physical substrate of brains – proved that non-formalist residue lingers even in the simplest formal systems such as arithmetic or numbers theory. Semantics, if you like, inheres in the mathematical syntax. More generally, semantics inheres in syntactic manipulations of symbols which, according to Searle, could never manifest themselves as consciousness or understanding.

But Gödel had one more surprise up his sleeve. In his last published paper, he showed that number theory *could* be shown to be consistent if one made certain very minimal assumptions about the *reality* of mathematical concepts, such as numbers or sets. Once again, it took a spectacular feat of metamathematical formalism to prove that reality will always waft in, no matter how frantically we try to slam the door on it.

Strange as it may appear, Gödel's rarefied, abstract, metamathematical formalism has something significant to say about evolution, namely that it is ineradicable from our thinking. Non-formalistic – in other words, this-worldly – "impurities" are ineradicably present even in our most formal systems of thought. This fits with Gödel's

Platonism (and the Platonic metaphysics of most mathematicians), insofar as Plato himself argued that our intuitive grasp of geometry demonstrates that we must harbour something of it within us.

In cognitive terms, Gödel proved that there is knowledge that cannot be fully formalized. Our knowledge of what is and what is true exceeds our capacity for proving it. We are the living proof of the incompleteness theorems: we know things we could not formalize, starting with the fact that induction works, which, deep down, is no more than an act of empirical faith.

Through trial by fire, errolution tests various adaptive solutions and organisms. Those that live on, whether amoebas or philosophers, *are* living theories about nature. What sets our own kind apart from other beings is the capacity for testing theories about nature without waiting for the patient hand of errolution. Human minds possess the capacity to drum up future-oriented scripts and update them in the course of hunting for a satisficing fit between fiction and fact.

Thought experiments are our best, cheapest tools for imagining and evaluating scenarios and states to see if they are worth pursuing. But, powerful as they are, thought experiments are subject to the same limitations as any other tool of the mind. Just as geometric intuitions can lead us astray outside what is evolutionarily true and tried, thought experiments and common sense in general fail outside the familiar scale and nature of events.

The death of two hundred million people is numerically two hundred times worse than the death of a million, yet emotionally we feel nothing of such escalating grief, except numbness in the face of hecatombs incomprehensible on the scale of a normal human life. Common sense fails as spectacularly in the realm of the very small. Wave-particle duality, quantum entanglement, and weak-force decay elude biologic that evolved to cope with medium-sized objects and events. Detecting patterns that harmonize with the world is inbred in our brains. But when it comes to what evolution put in our heads, some intuitions about patterns in the world are clearly more equal than others.

ROSENCRANTZ AND GUILDENSTERN

Probabilities are intuitions about uncertain outcomes or, if you like, uncertain intuitions about outcomes. How uncertain? You may think that in ten fair coin tosses, you are likely to end up with 5 heads and 5 tails, or at the most 6 and 4. In fact, it is more likely that you will end up with 7 and 3, or even 8 and 2. But, either way, if you flip ten heads or ten tails in a row, you will probably conclude that the coin is rigged.

Suppose, however, that instead of flipping just one coin, you pour out a bucket of them ten times in a row. Now it is practically certain that at least one will come up tails every time. What before looked like an anomalous piece of currency is now a nearly pre-destined outcome of the method itself (naturally, if the coin is balanced, subsequent tosses will almost certainly break the spell).

In general, the larger the total number of tosses – the larger the size of the statistical sample – the more likely it is that the relative frequencies will converge on half and half. At the same time, it is *more* likely that there will be longer and longer anomalous runs of non-stop heads or tails. This is exactly what makes the coin-tossing and destiny-driven (which is to say, probability-driven) film *Rosencrantz and Guildenstern Are Dead* so funny and so profound.

If our intuitions are tested by probabilities, the fault may lie as much with nature as with the non-intuitive way we have come to code them. As they are taught in school, frequencies of events are formalized in terms of the probability function of the probability calculus (technically, Bayesian inferences). This formalization is in contrast to natural frequencies that are expressed more intuitively as "one in x number of cases."

How we cope with statistical data often depends less on the data and more on how they are presented. When frequencies of events are cast in terms of the probability calculus, hacking through the formulae for base rates, hit rates, and false positive percentages proves a formidable obstacle for most of us, including trained professionals. When rearranged into natural frequencies, however, that same information begins to "talk," resulting in vastly superior performance.

To put it in plain language, people classify information and make predictions better when that information is put in plain language. In this case, plain language is the language of natural sampling, whereby people update event frequencies – plane crashes, hits by falling apples, mishaps on Fridays the thirteenth – from experience. Conversely, when probabilities are not expressed in this way, our processing capacities become stretched past their natural limit.

The case in point is a devastating blunder made by Alan Der-showitz while advising the defense team during O.J. Simpson's sensational 1995 criminal trial. Having misinterpreted the statistical correlation between wife battering and wife murder, the lawyer played it down as negligible, on the order of one in ten thousand, or a hundredth of 1 percent. Such low odds might indeed incline one to conclude that wife batterers are hardly killers. The truth, however, is shockingly different. The likelihood of a wife killer being a wife beater is 50 percent.

Expressed in natural frequencies, the reasoning is easy to follow. Every year, among ten thousand battered women, on average one is murdered by her husband and one by someone other than a husband. Thus two women from this group are likely to be killed every year, one of them by her spouse. This gives the probability of one in two that a battered, murdered wife has been killed by her husband, not 0.01 percent as claimed by Dershowitz.

Aided by evolution, we can, indeed, get something out of nothing. Recasting statistical evidence from the laboratory, the clinic, or the courtroom in terms of natural frequencies can make our minds smarter. This is because, when human minds come into play, information is not an independent quantity. Crucially, it depends on how it is represented. Most of us grasp this instinctively, in many cases systematizing, schematizing, and standardizing information far beyond the requirement of logical satisfiability.

All this is to say that, even if brains are minds, brains are more complex than minds – which is another way of saying that what we think *with* is more complex than what we think *about*. But the mental picture of the world registered by our minds harmonizes with what evolution has embedded in our brains, because, at the end of the day, we are talking about two sides of the same evolutionary coin.

11

Mind Your Business

100,000 Years; You're Flying Low, Mac; Neuromancer;
See Further; The Making of a Fly

100,000 YEARS

The information highway is a binary traffic system no different from
any other traffic system in at least one respect: it is insatiable. The
more highways we build, the more cars people buy and the more
congestion we see. It is the same in virtual space. The more broad-
band capacity that providers provide, the more Internet traffic
appears on the highway, necessitating an expansion of throughput
and storage which, in turn, brings in more traffic, more throughput, and so on, around and around.

A mere generation after the birth of the World Wide Web, the
quantity of information online far outstrips what any non-artificial
intelligence could fathom, even in a million years. Human sensory
and thus information-bearing capacities have, after all, remained
essentially unchanged for at least the last 100,000 years. We have
plugged the Stone Age brain straight into the Space Age, which
spawns information highways at an ever more frantic pace, burying
bigger and bigger massifs of data under even bigger and bigger
massifs of data.

Mining for information no longer resembles looking for the
proverbial needle in a haystack so much as looking for a sharp needle in the Himalayas of blunt ones. And the postmodem civilization of tomorrow will need all the help it can get in sorting out the
terabytes and then zettabytes of information sloshing back and
forth in cyberspace. How? We make prostheses that boost our physical capacities, from bulldozers that push urban trash around in

We have plugged the Stone Age brain straight into the Space Age, which spawns information highways at an ever more frantic pace, burying bigger and bigger massifs of data under even bigger and bigger massifs of data.

dumps to trash compactors. Why not mental prostheses in the form of Internet filters to sift out valuable data from cybertrash – for starters, where science and technology are concerned? (Things are, as always, a thousand times more gnarly when it comes to culture.)

It is guesstimated that up to 15 per cent of research undertaken worldwide is superfluous insofar as it duplicates work already been done by someone else. Informational filters that could liberate 15 per cent of brainpower on the global scale, even if this were their sole benefit, would be a windfall the consequences of which could hardly be overestimated. Our civilization would find itself in a position of a beleaguered general who gets a 15 per cent troop reinforcement in the heat of battle.

Of course, filtering data from among the quintillions of infobits that clog the Internet and its multifold incarnations, from YouTube to Google Scholar, has never posed much of a problem. But filtering valuable data is a different story, because to find what is valuable, we need to be able to evaluate what we find.

Borges spoofed the difference in one of his *ficciones* by compiling a brilliantly arbitrary bestiary, whereby animals are sorted out as follows: (a) those that belong to the Emperor, (b) embalmed ones, (c) those that are trained, (d) suckling pigs, (e) mermaids, (f) fabulous ones, (g) stray dogs, (h) those that are included in this classification, (i) those that tremble as if they were mad, (j) innumerable ones, (k) those drawn with a very fine camel's hair brush, (l) others, (m) those that have just broken a flower vase, and (n) those that resemble flies from a distance.

YOU'RE FLYING LOW, MAC

To filter out intelligence, you need intelligent filters. Searching by keyword, syntax, number of citations, or any other non-semantic parameter will never beat the results of an intelligent search for intelligence. Keywords cannot pick out a game-changer from a pool of bush leaguers who use the same lexicon. Syntax filters will identify correctly or complexly formulated sentences but will not spot a mastermind amongst mediocrity. Citation indices track not so much breakthrough thinking, which by default commands few adherents, as paradigm faddism and careerist genuflecting – scientists being no saintlier than the population at large.

Long story short, when it comes to mining data for signs of intelligence, nothing beats intelligence. Google puts millions of webpages at your fingertips in a split second, but it is up to you to access the first few hits (research shows that hardly anyone ventures past page 1), scan the contents, and determine if and how they are relevant to our search – something that the current generation of search bots is simply unable to do.

In 2011, Larry Page, chief executive of Google, acknowledged as much by remarking that the ultimate search engine would understand exactly what you mean and give back exactly what you want. Of course, to understand exactly what you mean, Internet intelligence will first need to get smart enough to parse intentions – smart enough, in other words, to pass the Turing test. Knowing this, Google, which has already invested a fortune and a half in AI, is leading the research into making search engines understand human-level, intention-based communication.

While it might appear that there could be communication without intentions, such as when DNA trades information with a habitat via an organism, this is not yet communication proper. The difference is crucial, roughly comparable to the difference between today's canned feedback that "Your Mac battery level is low" and tomorrow's computhor telling you something by clearing its throat, discreetly playing a sound of wings aflutter, and, if you still don't get it, whispering, "You're flying low, Mac."

Of course, Google is not alone in trying to make Internet filters smart and then some. DARPA, the European Union, and the WWW Consortium are all shovelling monies at Resource Description Framework (RDF) designed to encode and express meaning via Extensible Markup Language (XML). Their professed grail? The Semantic Web, capable of intuiting the intentions behind even vague queries and locating the right answer anywhere, in any language, in any form and medium.

NEUROMANCER

Fictions like *Neuromancer* like to dramatize the moment when artificial intelligence makes a leap into sentience and beyond. In Gibson's novel, the Turing Police vainly struggle to intercept a super-computer that plots to augment its intellectual capacities with a little help from a bunch of renegade hard-disc jockeys. In reality, the intelligence barrier will collapse without a bang or even a whisper.

Google will simply incrementally upgrade and finesse its search algorithms, eventually allowing users to pose questions and have answers enunciated in a language of their choice, as opposed to typing Boolean search terms and having reams of raw Internet pages spewed back. Somewhere on the way the search engines will begin to display intelligence just because they will have to in order to cope with vaguely phrased and open-ended queries.

As in the evolution of every business product, at first it will be merely a matter of making the search experience more enjoyable by letting users interact with a face animated on the screen, made attractive to the eye of the beholder by a suite of personalizable preferences and attuned to their search needs. "Beatles in Bangladesh?" you will type, and Victor or Victoria will smile, blink while scanning billions of documents in order to retrieve what you are after (you're writing a paper on entomology and not Band Aid), and recite the answer to you.

Later on, to make the results better and the interactive experience more satisfying, the search engine will try to anticipate what you may be looking for. Every Friday, for the past five weeks, you have browsed online sports listings for sailing events to watch on the weekend. One day Victoria will flash her perfect smile and, like the perfect service provider she is, ask you if it is going to be the usual. Gratefully, you will nod – it's been a hard week after your party has taken a beating in the polls – and off she goes to fetch the links to the roboat races you just asked for. Or did you?

Time passes, and gradually Victoria takes over other scheduling routines for you. And she excels in them. She never forgets that at the end of each month you need to run spreadsheets to calculate your expense accounts, that you need to run a spellcheck on the funding report for the congressional committee, that you run the risk of being decapitated if you do not send the anniversary card to your wife this Monday, and that you need to run to the pharmacy to get more headache pills, since the ones you bought online a month ago are running out.

With improvements in biometrics, Victoria – like everyone else, you have anthropomorphized the talking head or even torso, by now a three-dimensional plastiné artifact emoting back at you from your desktop – begins to take account of your moods as you bustle about your business. Not only does she correct the French accents that you always get wrong but she sympathizes with the pressures you are under to finish that controversial education reform paper. For a while now, she has been supplying you with *mots justes* better than anything you would have used in your policy drafts, and lately you have had her fix the solecisms in your introductions and conclusions which, as she knows, are always hardest to write.

SEE FURTHER

You could never pinpoint the moment when you started asking Victoria about piddling things, like where to find the cheapest cherry tomatoes of the kind you favour, or what garments to pack for the trip that will eventually prove as damp and rainy as she has gleaned from the forecasts you did not even consult. Why bother, when she does it better and faster? What is the most disaster-proof recipe for

There are matrimonial agencies doing brisk business bringing singles togeth-er, judicial courts where professional counsel is dispensed free of charge, confessionals that issue poignant solace and absolution, monetary and macro-economic policies that keep unemployment and inflation on the leash, inter-national tribunals that successfully arbitrate the beefs of all superpowers in a matter of seconds.

the flan you promised to bake for the twins' birthday? What is the best school to send the older kid to? How to get on the good side of that strutting incumbent?

One day, as you crack your head open over a forthcoming address that could determine your future in the party, Victoria comes up aces in the form of a draft that, you have to admit, is bril-liant. You bask in the plaudits, and next time you do not hesitate to solicit her help with that major policy memo. After all, no one will know where it came from and, besides, that competing analysis cir-culated by the opposition is nothing short of masterful, so much better than what anyone you know could write, including you. How did they ever come up with it?

Times passes. There are matrimonial agencies doing brisk busi-ness bringing singles together, judicial courts where professional counsel is dispensed free of charge, confessionals that issue poignant solace and absolution, monetary and macroeconomic policies that keep unemployment and inflation on the leash, international tribunals that successfully arbitrate the beefs of all superpowers in a matter of seconds. Human-run businesses and service providers have long since stopped trying to pass themselves off as AI, knowing they could never match the performance, not to mention that they would risk running afoul of penalties for deceiving the public.

The search engines that by now run all the affairs of the world, from federal governments to mortgage companies to local unions of pet-walkers, are intermeshed and at the same time dispersed around the globe. There is only one net, with every sensor and every processor plugged into it, with intelligence distributed over trillions of environment-monitoring, data-processing, and priority-negotiating individual nanocells and their fluid assemblies.

In this phase, a qualitatively new phenomenon will manifest itself on the planetary scale: the environment will have become more intelligent than its inhabitants. As such, it will exercise the prerogative of intelligence and override our individual and collective decisions, being able to see further, process faster, judge better, arbitrate more even-handedly, and legislate less corruptly – all the while in concert with our interests as *it* interprets them.

THE MAKING OF A FLY

What is going to happen when the Semantic Web eventually breaks out into the physical world, as inevitably it must if it is to perform the way we want it to? Is it going to prove itself equal to its physical – as opposed to merely informational – environment, or is it going to prove itself an experiential moron?

Algorithms may be cleverer than humans within their field of expertise, but they do not have our sense of perspective. This became spectacularly evident in 2011 when Amazon's price-setting code went to war with itself. *The Making of a Fly*, a book about the molecular biology of a fly from egg to fully fledged insect, may be a riveting read for some, but it hardly deserved a price tag of more than $23 million, which it reached after the algorithms used by Amazon to set and update prices started a bidding war against one another.

Such occasional stupidity notwithstanding, the future belongs to artificial intelligence. In 2011, Eric Schmidt, executive chairman of Google, made it very clear by hinting that in the future we will turn to a search engine to ask about which colleges to apply to or which books to read next. What then? Remember, you cannot have intelligence without the potential for self-modification under pressure from the environment, whether you call it learning or independent thinking.

Are Google's servers going to run bets on horse races on the side while taking and processing ours? Will the fifteen thousand networks distributed over seven million–plus devices registered to the US Department of Defense cunningly inflate the Pentagon networks budgets without anyone being the wiser? Will algo traders stash away the billions they will make trading for themselves in the wake of economic crashes and booms that succeed each other in the seven hundred trillion ocean of stocks, bonds, currencies, securities, and derivatives? Will they engineer financial markets meltdowns because that is when the biggest fortunes are made?

Idle speculation? Consider what happened in May 2010 when the Dow Jones nosedived six hundred points in five minutes for no apparent reason whatsoever. Why did it do so, and why ten minutes after that did it go back up again? To this day analysts scratch their heads as to what happened. The only thing they agree on is that the "flash crash" had something to do with the algorithms.

Still sceptical? In August 2012, equipped with a new, albeit thoroughly tested trading algorithm, Knight Capital linked up to the New York Stock Exchange intending to make a killing. The instant it went online, something went spectacularly wrong, although to this day no one knows exactly what. From the outside it looked as if the meticulously tested program went loco, buying *high* and selling *low* thousands of times a second. When it was ditched at the end of forty-five minutes, the company was almost half a billion in the red.

One thing is certain: if algos ever go native, no amount of Turing policing will stop them.

Notes

LEMMATA

1 Solotaroff, "Genius of Stanislaw Lem," 186.

CHAPTER ONE

1 Lem, *Imaginary Magnitude*, 41.
2 The second is from Baudrillard.
3 In Simons, *Are Computers Alive*, 71.
4 Chamberlain, http://www.atariarchives.org/deli/write_about
   _itself.php.
5 Ibid.
6 Poe, *Tales of the Grotesque*, vol. 1, 339, 343.

CHAPTER TWO

1 Lem, "History of Bitic Literature," 47.
2 Ibid., 58.
3 Reprinted in Bowden, *Faster than Thought*, 398.
4 Peat, *Artificial Intelligence*, 311.

CHAPTER THREE

1 Lem, "History of Bitic Literature," 42.
2 Michie and Johnston, *Creative Computer*, 71.
3 Wakefield, "When Algorithms Control the World."
4 Cohen, "Colouring without Seeing."
5 Franke, *Computer Graphics, Computer Art*, 119.

CHAPTER FOUR

1 *Graham's Magazine*, May 1842.
2 Peggy Kamuf, in Kelly, *Encyclopedia of Aesthetics*, vol. 2, 11.

CHAPTER FIVE

1 Colby et al., "Turing-Like Indistinguishability Tests," 202.
2 Turing, "Computing Machinery and Intelligence," 13.
3 Jacquette, "Who's Afraid of the Turing Test?," 64.
4 McCulloch, "Mysterium Iniquitatis," 36.
5 "Computing Machinery and Intelligence," 14.
6 Dennett, "Fast Thinking," 334.

CHAPTER SIX

1 Searle, *Mystery of Consciousness*, 61.
2 Hofstadter, *I Am a Strange Loop*, 30.
3 Simon and Newall, "Heuristic Problem Solving," 1–10.
4 In Copeland, *The Essential Turing*, 407.
5 Millar, "On the Point of the Imitation Game," 595; Block, "Troubles," 248, Hodges, *Alan Turing*, 415.
6 French, "The Turing Test," 115; Prager, *On Turing*, 45.
7 In Copeland, *The Essential Turing*, 494.
8 Turing, "Computing Machinery and Intelligence," 14.
9 French, "Subcognition and the Limits of the Turing Test," 59.

CHAPTER SEVEN

1 McCorduck, *Machines Who Think*, 464.
2 Ibid.
3 Weizenbaum, *Computer Power and Human Reason*, 10
4 Tomasello, *Origins of Human Communication*, 134.
5 McCarthy, "Problems and Projections," 615.

CHAPTER EIGHT

1 Hayles, *Electronic Literature*, 47; Shurkin, "Expert Systems," 72.
2 Turkle, *Life on the Screen*; Benford and Malartre, *Beyond Human*.
3 Simons, *Are Computers Alive*, 14.

4 Ibid., 17.

5 Ibid., x.

6 Ibid., 109.

7 Ibid., 22.

8 "Software für die Seele" (Software for the soul), *Der Spiegel*, 5 September 1994, 116.

9 Fitzpatrick, "No, Robot."

Bibliography

Aarseth, Espen J. *Cybertext: Perspectives on Ergodic Literature.* Baltimore, MD: Johns Hopkins University Press 1997.

Aitchison, Jean. *The Seeds of Speech: Language Origin and Evolution.* Cambridge: Cambridge University Press 2000.

Allen, Robert F. "The Stylo-Statistical Method of Literary Analysis." *Computers and the Humanities* 22 (1988): 1–10.

Anderson, Alan Ross, ed. *Minds and Machines.* Englewood Cliffs, NJ: Prentice-Hall 1964.

Ayer, Alfred J. *Language, Truth and Logic.* London: Victor Gollancz 1936.

Barbrook, Adrian C., Christopher J. Howe, Norman Blake, and Peter Robinson. "The Phylogeny of *The Canterbury Tales.*" *Nature* 394 (27 August 1998): 839.

Baron-Cohen, Simon. "The Empathizing System: A Revision of the 1994 Model of the Mindreading System." In *Origins of the Social Mind: Evolutionary Psychology and Child Development,* edited by Bruce J. Ellis and David F. Bjorklund, 468–92. New York: Guilford 2005.

Baron-Cohen, Simon, Helen Tager-Flusberg, and Donald J. Cohen, eds. *Understanding Other Minds: Perspectives from Developmental and Cognitive Neuroscience.* 2nd ed. Oxford: Oxford University Press 2000.

Baudrillard, Jean. "Simulacra and Simulations." In *Jean Baudrillard, Selected Writings,* edited by Mark Poster, 166–84. Stanford: Stanford University Press 1998.

BBC. "IBM Researchers Make 12-Atom Magnetic Memory Bit." 13 January 2012. http://www.bbc.co.uk/news/technology-16543497.

Bedau, Mark A., and Paul Humphreys, eds. *Emergence: Contemporary Readings in Philosophy and Science.* Cambridge, MA: MIT Press 2008.

Behne, T., M. Carpenter, J. Call, and M. Tomasello. "Unwilling versus

Unable? Infants' Understanding of Intentional Action." *Developmental Psychology* 41 (2005): 328–37.

Behne, T., M. Carpenter, and M. Tomasello. "One-Year-Olds Comprehend the Communicative Intentions behind Gestures in a Hiding Game." *Developmental Science* 8 (2005): 492–9.

Benford, Gregory, and Elisabeth Malartre. *Beyond Human: Living with Robots and Cyborgs.* New York: Forge Books 2007.

Bennett, Maxwell, Deniel C. Dennett, Peter Hacker, and John Searle. *Neuroscience and Philosophy: Brains, Minds, and Language.* New York: Columbia University Press 2009.

Bernal, J.D. *The Origins of Life.* London: Weidenfeld & Nicholson 1967.

Berrill, Norman John. *Biology in Action.* London: Heinemann 1966.

Block, Ned. "Troubles with Functionalism." In *Perception and Cognition: Issues in the Foundations of Psychology,* edited by C.W. Savage. Vol. 9. Minneapolis: University of Minnesota Press 1978.

– "The Computer Model of the Mind." In *Thinking,* edited by D.N. Osherson and H. Lasnik. Vol. 3, *An Invitation to Cognitive Science.* Cambridge, MA: MIT Press 1990.

Boden, Margaret A. *Artificial Intelligence and Natural Man.* Brighton: Harvester 1977.

– *Mind as Machine: A History of Cognitive Science.* Oxford: Oxford University Press 2006.

Bolton, W.F. "A Poetic Formula in Beowulf and Seven Other Old English Poems: A Computer Study." *Computers and the Humanities* 19 (1985): 167–73.

Borges, Jorge Luis. "The Analytical Language of John Wilkins." *Other Inquisitions, 1937–1952.* Translated by Ruth L.C. Simms. Austin: University of Texas Press 1993.

Bowden, B.V., ed. *Faster than Thought: A Symposium on Digital Computing Machines.* New York: Pitman 1953.

Bratman, Michael. "Shared Co-Operative Activity." *Philosophical Review* 101 (1992): 327–41.

Bruner, Jerome. *Child's Talk.* New York: Norton 1983.

Budiansky, Stephen. *If a Lion Could Talk: How Animals Think.* London: Weidenfeld & Nicolson 1998.

Burrows, John F. "Computers and the Study of Literature." In *Computers and Written Texts,* edited by Christopher Butler. Oxford: Blackwell 1992.

Buss, David M. *Evolutionary Psychology: The New Science of the Mind.* Boston: Allyn & Bacon 1999.

Cacioppo, John T., and William Patrick. *Loneliness: Human Nature and the Need for Social Connection*. New York: Norton 2008.

Camerer, Colin, George Lowenstein, and Drazen Prelec. "Neuroeconomics: How Neuroscience Can Inform Economics." *Journal of Economic Literature* 43 (2005): 9–64.

Caras, Pauline. "Literature and Computers: A Short Bibliography, 1980–1987." *College Literature* 15 (1988): 69–82.

Carroll, Lewis. *Symbolic Logic*. London: Macmillan 1896.

Ceruzzi, Paul E. *Reckoners: The Prehistory of the Digital Computer, from Relays to the Stored Program Concept, 1935–1945*. Westport, CT: Greenwood Press 1983.

Chamberlain, Bill. "Getting a Computer to Write about Itself." 1984. http://www.atariarchives.org/deli/write_about_itself.php.

Charabia. http://www.charabia.net/gen/index.php.

Christian, Brian. *The Most Human Human: What Talking with Computers Teaches Us about What It Means to Be Alive*. New York: Doubleday 2011.

Clark, Herbert. *Using Language*. Cambridge: Cambridge University Press 1996.

Clarke, David S. *Panpsychism and the Religious Attitude*. Albany, NY: SUNY Press 2003.

– ed. *Panpsychism: Past and Recent Selected Readings*. Albany, NY: SUNY Press 2004.

Cohen, Gillian. *The Psychology of Cognition*. London: Academic 1977.

Cohen, Harold. "Colouring without Seeing: A Problem in Machine Creativity." (1999). http://www.aaronshome.com/aaron/publications/colouringwithoutseeing.pdf.

Cohen, Paul R. "If Not Turing's Test, Then What?" *AI Magazine* 26, no. 4 (2006). http://www.cs.arizona.edu/~cohen/Publications/papers/IfNotWhat.pdf.

Colby, Kenneth M. "Modeling a Paranoid Mind." *Behavioural and Brain Sciences* 4 (1981): 515–60.

Colby, Kenneth M., and Robert J. Stoller. *Cognitive Science and Psychoanalysis*. New York and London: Routledge 1988.

Colby, Kenneth M., F.D. Hilf, S. Weber, and H.C. Kraemer. "Turing-Like Indistinguishability Tests for the Validation of Computer Simulation of Paranoid Processes." *Artificial Intelligence* 3 (1972): 199–221.

Collins, H.M. *Artificial Experts: Social Knowledge and Intelligent Machines*. Cambridge, MA: MIT Press 1990.

Collins, Nick. *Introduction to Computer Music*. Chichester: Wiley 2009.

Conway, John H. *On Numbers and Games.* 2nd ed. Wellesley, MA: A.K. Peters 2001.

Copeland, B. Jack., ed. *The Essential Turing: The Ideas That Gave Birth to the Computer Age.* Oxford: Oxford University Press 2004.

Corns, Thomas N., and Margarette E. Smith. "Computers in the Humanities: Methods and Applications in the Study of English Literature." *Literary and Linguistic Computing* 6 (1991): 127–30.

– "Literature." In *Information Technology in the Humanities: Tools, Techniques, and Applications,* edited by Sebastian Rahtz. Chichester, NY: Wiley 1987.

Damasio, Antonio. *Looking for Spinoza: Joy, Sorrow, and the Feeling Brain.* Orlando, FL: Harcourt 2003.

Davidson, Donald. "Mental Events." In *Experience and Theory,* edited by L. Foster and J. Swanson. London: Duckworth 1970.

Deacon, Terrence. *The Symbolic Species: The Co-Evolution of Language and the Human Brain.* London: Penguin 1997.

de la Mettrie, Julien Offray. *Machine Man and Other Writings.* Translated by Ann Thomson. Cambridge: Cambridge University Press 1996.

Dennett, C. Daniel. *Consciousness Explained.* Boston: Little, Brown 1991.

– "Fast Thinking." *The Intentional Stance.* Cambridge, MA: MIT Press 1987.

De Waal, Frans. *The Age of Empathy: Nature's Lessons for a Kinder Society.* New York: Crown 2009.

Dimberg, U., M. Thunberg, and K. Elmehed. "Unconscious Facial Reactions to Emotional Facial Expressions." *Psychological Science* 11 (2000): 86–9.

Dreyfus, Hubert. *What Computers Can't Do: A Critique of Artificial Reason.* New York: Harper & Row 1972.

– *What Computers Still Can't Do.* Cambridge, MA: MIT Press 1979.

Dunbar, Robin, and Louise Barrett. *Oxford Handbook of Evolutionary Psychology.* New York: Oxford University Press 2007.

Dyson, George. *Darwin among the Machines: The Evolution of Global Intelligence.* New York: Basic 1998.

Eco, Umberto. *Baudolino.* San Diego: Harcourt 2000.

Economist, The. "Can Machines Surpass Humans in Intelligence?" 12 March 2011, 86.

– "Intelligence Testing: Who Are You Calling Bird-Brained?" 5 March 2011, 79.

– "Painting by Numbers." 30 July 2011, 67.

Edelman, Gerald M. *Bright Air, Brilliant Fire.* New York: Basic 1992.

Enfield, N.J., and Stephen C. Levinson, eds. *Roots of Human Sociality: Culture, Cognition and Interaction*. Oxford: Berg 2006.

Enriquez, Juan, and Steve Gullans. *Homo Evolutis*. Amazon Media: Kindlebook 2011.

Farley, B.G., and W.A. Clark. "Simulation of Self-Organizing Systems by Digital Computer." *Institute of Radio Engineers Transactions on Information Theory* 4 (1954): 76–84.

Feigenbaum, Edward A. "Some Challenges and Grand Challenges for Computational Intelligence." *Journal of the ACM* 50, no. 1 (2003): 32–40.

Fitzpatrick, Michael. "No, Robot: Japan's Elderly Fail to Welcome Their Robot Overlords." 4 February 2011. http://www.bbc.co.uk/news/business-12347219.

Focquaert, Farah, and Steven M. Platek. "Social Cognition and the Evolution of Self-Awareness." In *Evolutionary Cognitive Neuroscience*, edited by Steven M. Platek, Julian Paul Keenan, and Todd K. Shackelford, 457–97. Cambridge, MA: MIT Press 2007.

Fortier, Paul A. "Theory and Practice in the Use of Computers for the Study of Literature." In *Actes du VIIIe Congres de l'Association Internationale de Litterature Comparee/Proceedings of the 8th Congress of the International Comparative Literature Association*, edited by Bela Kopeczi and Gyorgy M. Vajda. Stuttgart: Bieber 1980.

Franke, Herbert W. *Computer Graphics, Computer Art*. Translated by Gustav Metzger. New York: Phaidon 1971.

Freeman, Anthony, ed. *Consciousness and Its Place in Nature: Does Physicalism Entail Panpsychism?* Exeter: Imprint Academic 2006.

French, Robert M. "Subcognition and the Limits of the Turing Test." *Mind* 99 (1990): 53–65.

– "The Turing Test: The First 50 Years." *Trends in Cognitive Sciences* 4 (2000): 115–22.

Gardner, Howard. *Frames of Mind: The Theory of Multiple Intelligences*. New York: Basic 1983.

Genova, J. "Turing's Sexual Guessing Game." *Social Epistemology* 8, no. 4 (1994): 314–26.

Gibson, William *Neuromancer*. London: Victor Gollancz 1984

Gödel, Kurt. *Collected Works*. Vol. 2, *Publications, 1938–1974*. Oxford: Oxford University Press 1990.

Goleman, Daniel. *Social Intelligence: The New Science of Human Relationships*. New York: Arrow 2007.

Gomez, Juan-Carlos. "The Emergence of Intentional Communication as a Problem-Solving Strategy in the Gorilla." In *"Language" and Intelligence in Monkeys and Apes*, edited by S.T. Parker and K.R. Gibson. Cambridge: Cambridge University Press 1990.

– *Apes, Monkeys, Children, and the Growth of Mind*. Cambridge, MA: Harvard University Press 2004.

Gopnik, Alison. *The Philosophical Baby: What Children's Minds Tell Us about Truth, Love, and the Meaning of Life*. New York: Farrar, Straus and Giroux 2009.

Gregory, Richard, and Pauline K. Marstrand, eds. *Creative Intelligence*. Norwood, NJ: Ablex 1987.

Gurewich, David. "Games Computers Play." *New Criterion* 7 (1989): 81–4.

Harnad, Stevan. "The Annotation Game: On Turing (1950) on Computing, Machinery, and Intelligence." In *The Turing Test Sourcebook: Philosophical and Methodological Issues in the Quest for the Thinking Computer*, edited by Robert Epstein and Grace Peters. Dordrecht and Boston: Kluwer 2004.

Haugeland, John, ed. *Mind Design*. Cambridge, MA: MIT Press 1981.

Hayes, Patrick, and Kenneth Ford. "Turing Test Considered Harmful." In *Proceedings of the Fourteenth International Joint Conference on Artificial Intelligence*, 972–97. San Francisco: Morgan Kaufmann 1995.

Hayles, Katherine. *Electronic Literature: New Horizons for the Literary*. Notre Dame, IN: University of Notre Dame Press 2008.

Heil, John. *Philosophy of Mind: A Contemporary Introduction*. London and New York: Routledge 1998.

Henrich, Joseph, Robert Boyd, Samuel Bowles, Colin Camerer, Ernst Fehr, Herbert Gintis, Richard McElreath, Michael Alvard, Abigail Barr, Jean Ensminger, Kim Hill, Francisco Gil-White, Michael Gurven, Frank Marlowe, John Q. Patton, Natalie Smith, and David Tracer. "'Economic Man' in Cross-Cultural Perspective: Ethnography and Experiments from Fifteen Small-Scale Societies." *Behavioral and Brain Sciences* 28 (2005): 795–855.

Hernandez-Orallo, Jose. "Beyond the Turing Test." *Journal of Logic, Language and Information* 9, no. 4 (2000): 447–66.

Hernandez-Orallo, Jose, and D.L. Dowe. "Measuring Universal Intelligence: Towards an Anytime Intelligence Test." *Artificial Intelligence Journal* 174 (2010): 1508–39.

Hodges, Andrew. *Alan Turing: The Enigma*. New York: Simon & Schuster 1983.

Hoffman, Elizabeth, Kevin McCabe, and Vernon L. Smith. "On Expectations and the Monetary Stakes in Ultimatum Games." *International Journal of Game Theory* 25 (1996): 289–301.

Hofstadter, Douglas R. *Gödel, Escher, Bach: An Eternal Golden Braid.* New York: Vintage 1979.

– *I Am a Strange Loop.* New York: Basic 2007.

Hofstadter, Douglas R., and Daniel C. Dennett, eds. *The Mind's I: Fantasies and Reflections on Self and Soul.* New York: Basic 1981.

Horn, William Dennis. "The Effect of the Computer on the Written Word." In *Sixth International Conference on Computers and the Humanities,* edited by Sarah K. Burton and Douglas D. Short. Rockville, MD: Computer Science Press 1983.

Horowitz, Irving Louis. "Printed Words, Computers and Democratic Societies." *Virginia Quarterly Review* 59 (1983): 620–36.

Iacoboni, Marco. *Mirroring People: The Science of Empathy and How We Connect with Others.* New York: Picador 2008.

Ide, Nancy M. "A Statistical Measure of Theme and Structure." *Computers and the Humanities* 23 (1989): 277–83.

ITRS: International Technology Roadmap for Semiconductors. 2012. http://www.itrs.net/.

Jacquette, Dale. "Who's Afraid of the Turing Test?" *Behavior and Philosophy* 20/21 (1993): 63–74.

Kahneman, Daniel. *Thinking, Fast and Slow.* New York: Farrar, Straus & Giroux 2011.

Kasparov, Gary. "The Day That I Sensed a New Kind of Intelligence." *Time,* 1 April 1996, 57.

Kauffman, Stuart A. *At Home in the Universe: The Search for Laws of Self-Organization and Complexity.* Oxford: Oxford University Press 1995.

– *Reinventing the Sacred: A New View of Science, Reason and Religion.* New York: Basic 2008.

Kelly, Michael, ed. *Encyclopedia of Aesthetics.* 4 vols. New York: Oxford University Press 1998.

Keltner, Dacher. *Born to Be Good: The Science of a Meaningful Life.* New York: W.W. Norton 2009.

Kern, Alfred, and James F. Sheridan. "BASIC Poetry: The Computer as Poet." In *Sixth International Conference on Computers and the Humanities,* edited by Sarah K. Burton and Douglas D. Short. Rockville, MD: Computer Science Press 1983.

Kurzweil, Ray. *The Age of Intelligent Machines.* Cambridge, MA: MIT Press 1990.

– *The Singularity Is Near*. London: Penguin 2005.

Kybernetes 4 (April 2010). Special Turing issue.

Leavitt, David. *The Man Who Knew Too Much: Alan Turing and the Invention of the Computer*. New York: Norton 2006.

Leebaert, Derek, ed. *Technology 2001: The Future of Computing and Communications*. Cambridge, MA: MIT Press 1991.

Legg, Shane, and Marcus Hutter. "Universal Intelligence: A Definition of Machine Intelligence." *Minds and Machines* 17, no. 4 (2007): 391–444.

Lem, Stanislaw. *Bomba megabitowa*. Cracow: Wydawnictwo Literackie 1999.

– "A History of Bitic Literature." *Imaginary Magnitude*. Translated by Marc E. Heine. San Diego: Harcourt 1985.

– *Perfect Vacuum*. Translated by Michael Kandel. Evanston, IL: Northwestern University Press 1971.

– "Smart Robots." In *The Art and Science of Stanislaw Lem*, edited by Peter Swirski. Montreal and London: McGill-Queen's University Press 2006.

– *Solaris*. Translated by Joanna Kilmartin and Steve Cox. New York: Walker & Co. 1971.

– *Summa technologiae*. Cracow: Wydawnictwo Literackie 1971.

– *Tajemnica chińskiego pokoju*. Cracow: Universitas 1996.

Lenat, Douglas. "Eurisco: A Program That Learns New Heuristics and Domain Concepts." *Artificial Intelligence* 21 (March 1983): 61–98.

Levy, David. *Love and Sex with Robots: The Evolution of Human-Robot Relationships*. New York: Harper Perennial 2007.

Liszkowski, Ulf. "Human Twelve-Month-Olds Point Co-operatively to Share Interest and Provide Information for a Communicative Partner." *Gesture* 5 (2005): 135–54.

– "Infant Pointing at Twelve Months: Communicative Goals, Motives, and Social-Cognitive Abilities." In *Roots of Human Sociality: Culture, Cognition and Interaction*, edited by Nicholas J. Enfield and Stephen C. Levinson. Oxford: Berg 2006.

Lucas, John R. "Minds, Machines, and Gödel." In *Minds and Machines*, edited by Alan Ross Anderson. Englewood Cliffs, NJ: Prentice-Hall 1964.

Lupkowski, Pawel. "Some Historical Remarks on Block's 'Aunt Bubbles' Argument." *Mind and Machines* 16, no. 4 (2006): 437–41.

Lycan, William G. *Consciousness*. Cambridge, MA: MIT Press 1995.

– *Consciousness and Experience*. Cambridge, MA: MIT Press 1996.

– ed. *Mind and Cognition: An Anthology.* 2nd ed. Maiden, MA: Blackwell 1999.

Manning, Peter. *Electronic and Computer Music.* Oxford: Oxford University Press 2004.

Marcus, Stephen. "Computers and the Poetic Muse." In *Sixth International Conference on Computers and the Humanities,* edited by Sarah K. Burton and Douglas D. Short. Rockville, MD: Computer Science Press 1983.

McCarthy, John. "Problems and Projections in CS for the Next Forty-Nine Years." *Journal of the ACM* 50, no. 1 (2003): 73–9.

– "Programs with Common Sense." *Symposium on Mechanization of Thought Processes.* National Physical Laboratory, Teddington, UK, 1958. http://www-formal.stanford.edu/jmc/mcc59.pdf.

– "Review of *The Emperor's New Mind* by Roger Penrose." *Bulletin of the American Mathematical Society* 23 (October 1990): 606–16.

McCorduck, Pamela. *Machines Who Think.* 2nd ed. Wellesley, MA: A.K. Peters 2004.

McCullouch, Warren S. "Mysterium Iniquitatis of Sinful Man Aspiring into the Place of God." *Scientific Monthly* 80, no. 1 (1955): 35–9.

Meehan, James R. "Tale-Spin, an Interactive Program That Writes Stories." In *Proceedings of the Fifth International Conference on Artificial Intelligence.* Vol. 1. Pittsburg: Carnegie-Mellon University Department of Science, 1977.

Melpomene [G.E. Hughes]. *Bagabone, Hem 'I Die Now.* New York: Vantage 1980.

Michie, Donald. *On Machine Intelligence.* 2nd ed. Chichester: Ellis Horwood 1986.

– *On Machine Intelligence, Biology and More,* edited by Ashwin Sriniwasan. Oxford: Oxford University Press 2009.

Michie, Donald, and Rory Johnston. *The Creative Computer: Machine Intelligence and Human Knowledge.* Harmondsworth: Viking 1984.

Millar, P.H. "On the Point of the Imitation Game." *Mind* 82 (1973): 595–7.

Miller, Richard. *Fact and Method: Explanation, Confirmation and Reality in the Natural and the Social Sciences.* Princeton: Princeton University Press 1987.

Millican, Peter, and Andy Clark, eds. *Machines and Thought: The Legacy of Alan Turing.* Vol. 1. Oxford: Oxford University Press 1996.

Minsky, Marvin. "Why People Think Computers Can't." *AI Magazine* (Fall 1982): 3–15.

Mitchell, T.M. *Machine Learning.* New York: McGraw-Hill 1997.

Moor, James H. "An Analysis of the Turing Test." *Philosophical Studies* 30 (1976): 249–57.

– "The Status and Future of the Turing Test." *Minds and Machines* 11, no. 1 (2001): 77–93.

– ed. *The Turing Test: The Elusive Standard of Artificial Intelligence.* Dordrecht: Kluwer 2003.

Moravec, Hans. *Mind Children: The Future of Robot and Human Intelligence.* Cambridge, MA: Harvard University Press 1988.

– *Robot: Mere Machine to Transcendent Mind.* New York: Oxford University Press 1998.

Munz, Peter. *Philosophical Darwinism: On the Origin of Knowledge by Means of Natural Selection.* New York and London: Routledge 1993.

Negroponte, Nicholas. "The Return of the Sunday Painter." In *The Computer Age: A Twenty-Year View,* edited by Michael Dertouzos and Joel Moses. Cambridge, MA: MIT Press 1979.

Neumaier, O. "A Wittgensteinian View of Artificial Intelligence." In *Artificial Intelligence: The Case Against.*, edited by Reiner Born. London: Croom Helm 1987.

Niesz, Anthony J., and Normal N. Holland. "Interactive Fiction." *Critical Inquiry* 11 (1984): 110–29.

Northcott, Bryan. "But Is It Mozart?" *The Independent.* 5 September 1997. http://www.independent.co.uk/arts-entertainment/music/but-is-it-mozart-1237509.html.

Ochs, E.P., M. Meana, K. Mah, and Y.M. Binik. "The Effects of Exposure to Different Sources of Sexual Information on Sexual Behaviour: Comparing a 'Sex-Expert System' to Other Educational Material." *Behavioural Research Methods, Instruments, and Computers* 25 (1993): 189–94.

Ochs, E.P., M. Meana, L. Pare, K. Mah, and Y.M. Binik. "Learning about Sex outside the Gutter: Attitudes toward a Computer Sex-Expert System." *Journal of Sex and Marital Therapy* 20 (1994): 86–102.

Peat, F. David. *Artificial Intelligence: How Machines Think.* New York: Bean 1988.

Peer, Willie van. "Quantitative Studies of Literature: A Critique and an Outlook." *Computers and the Humanities* 23 (1989): 301–7.

Perry, Mark, and Thomas Margoni. "From Music Tracks to Google Maps: Who Owns Computer-Generated Works?" *Computer Law and Security Review* 26 (2010): 621–9.

Petzold, Charles. *The Annotated Turing: A Guided Tour through Alan Turing's Historic Paper on Computability and the Turing Machine.* Indianapolis: Wiley & Sons 2008.

Pihlström, Sami. *Jamesian Perspectives on Mind, World, and Religion.* Lanham, MD: University Press of America 2008.

Poe, Edgar Allan. "The Philosophy of Composition." Orig. 1846. In *The Complete Works of Edgar Allan Poe,* edited by J.A. Harrison, vol. 14, 193–208. New York: T.Y. Crowell 1902.

– *Tales of the Grotesque and Arabesque.* 2 vols. Philadelphia: Lea and Blanchard 1840.

– "Twice-Told Tales: A Review." *Graham's Magazine* (Philadelphia), May 1842.

Potter, Rosanne G. "Statistical Analysis of Literature: A Retrospective on Computers and the Humanities, 1966–1990." *Computers and the Humanities* 25 (1991): 401–29.

Poundstone, William. *The Recursive Universe: Cosmic Complexity and the Limits of Scientific Knowledge.* Oxford: Oxford University Press 1987.

Prager, John. *On Turing.* Belmont, CA: Wadsworth 2001.

Premack, David, and Ann James Premack. "Origins of Human Social Competence." In *The Cognitive Neurosciences,* edited by Michael S. Gazzaniga, 205–18. Cambridge, MA: MIT Press 1995.

Quine, Willard von. *Word and Object.* Cambridge, MA: MIT Press 1960.

Racter. *Endangered Software Archive.* http://www.mirrors.org/archived _software/www.techknight.com/esa/default.htm.

Racter [William Chamberlain and Thomas Etter]. *The Policeman's Beard Is Half Constructed.* New York: Warner 1984.

Rizzolatti, Giacomo, and Leonardo Fogassi. "Mirror Neurons and Social Cognition." In *Oxford Handbook of Evolutionary Psychology,* edited by Robin Dunbar and Louise Barrett, 179–95. New York: Oxford University Press 2007.

Robinson, William S. *Computers, Minds and Robots.* Philadelphia: Temple University Press 1992.

Roland, Alex, with Philip Shiman. *Strategic Computing: DARPA and the Quest for Machine Intelligence.* Cambridge, MA: MIT Press 2002.

Roper, John P.G., ed. *Computers in Literary and Linguistic Research.* Paris: Champion 1988.

Russell, Stuart J., and Peter Norvig. *Artificial Intelligence: A Modern Approach.* 2nd ed. Upper Saddle River, NJ: Prentice Hall 2003.

Sanfey, Alan G., James K. Rilling, Jessica A. Aaronson, Leigh E. Nystrom, and Jonathan D. Cohen. "The Neural Basis of Economic Decision-Making in the Ultimatum Game." *Science* 300 (2003): 1755–8.

Saxby, Steven. *The Age of Information.* New York: New York University Press 1990.

Saygin, Ayse P. "Comments on 'Computing Machinery and Intelligence' by Alan Turing." In *Parsing the Turing Test,* edited by R. Epstein, G. Roberts, and G. Poland. Dordrecht: Springer 2008.

Saygin, Ayse P., and Ilyas Cicekli. "Pragmatics in Human-Computer Conversation." *Journal of Pragmatics* 34, no. 3 (2002): 227–58.

Saygin, Ayse P., I. Cicekli, and V. Akman. "Turing Test: 50 Years Later." *Minds and Machines* 10, no. 4 (2000): 463–518.

Schaffer, Simon. "Making Up Discovery." In *Dimensions of Creativity,* edited by Margaret Boden, 13–51. Cambridge, MA: MIT Press 1994.

Schank, Roger C. *Dynamic Memory: A Theory of Reminding and Learning in Computers and People.* Cambridge: Cambridge University Press 1982.

Schwartz, Richard Alan. "New Possibilities for Computer Literature." In *Sixth International Conference on Computers and the Humanities,* edited by Sarah K. Burton and Douglas D. Short. Rockville, MD: Computer.Science Press 1983.

Seager, William. "Consciousness, Information and Panpsychism." In *Explaining Consciousness,* edited by J. Shear. Cambridge, MA: MIT Press 1997.

Searle, John. *The Construction of Social Reality.* New York: Free Press 1995.

– "Minds, Brains, and Programs." *Behavioral and Brain Sciences* 3 (1980): 417–57.

– *Minds, Brains, and Science.* Cambridge, MA: Harvard University Press 1984.

– *The Mystery of Consciousness.* New York: New York Review of Books 1997.

Shah, Huma. "Turing's Misunderstood Imitation Game and IBM's Watson Success." http://reading.academia.edu/HumaShah/Papers/464364/Turings_misunderstood_imitation_game_and_IBMs_Watson_success.

Shieber, Stuart M. "Lessons from a Restricted Turing Test." *Communications of the ACM* 37, no. 6 (1994): 70–8.

Shiels Maggie. "Google Enters Digital Books War." 5 May 2010. http://www.bbc.co.uk/news/10098111.

Shurkin, Joel. *Engines of the Mind: A History of the Computer.* New York: Norton 1984.

– "Expert Systems: The Practical Face of Artificial intelligence." *Technology Review* 86 (1983): 72–7.

Simon, Herbert A., and Allen Newall. "Heuristic Problem Solving: The Next Advance in Operations Research." *Operations Research* 6 (1958): 1–10.

Simons, Geoff. *Are Computers Alive: Evolution and New Life Forms.* Boston: Birkhäuser 1983.

Skrbina, David. *Panpsychism in the West.* Cambridge, MA: MIT Press 2005.

Smith, Paul. "The Joke Machine: Communicating Traditional Humour Using Computers." In *Spoken in Jest,* edited by Gillian Bennett. Sheffield: Sheffield Academy Press 1991.

Sober, Elliott, and David Sloan Wilson. *Unto Others: The Evolution and Psychology of Unselfish Behavior.* New York: Dutton 1999.

Solotaroff, Theodore. "The Genius of Stanislaw Lem." *A Few Good Voices in My Head.* New York: Harper & Row 1987.

Sorensen, Alan, Jonah Berger, and Scott Rasmussen. "Positive Effects of Negative Publicity: Can Negative Reviews Increase Sales?" *Marketing Science* 29 (2010): 5. http://www.stanford.edu/~asorense/papers/Negative_Publicity2.pdf.

Spiegel, Der. "Software für die Seele." 5 September 1994, 116–18.

Stine, G. Harry. *The Untold Story of the Computer Revolution.* New York: Arbour 1985.

Stone, Valerie E. "Theory of Mind and the Evolution of Social Intelligence." *Social Neuroscience: People Thinking about People,* edited by John T. Cacioppo, Penny S. Visser, and Cynthia L. Pickett, 103–30. Cambridge, MA: Bradford-MIT Press 2006.

Swirski, Peter, ed. *The Art and Science of Stanislaw Lem.* Montreal, London: McGill-Queen's University Press 2006.

– "*Cogito Ergo Scribo*: Stanislaw Lem and Evolution." In *The Evolutionary Review: Art, Science and Culture,* edited by Alice Andrews and Michelle Scalise Sugiyama. New York: SUNY Press 2012.

– "Computhors and Biterature: Machine-Written Fiction?" *SubStance* 70 (1993): 81–90.

– *Lem: Polemics: Essays, Letters, and Provocation.* Montreal and London: McGill-Queen's University Press 2013.

– *Literature, Analytically Speaking: Explorations in the Theory of Interpretation, Analytic Aesthetics, and Evolution (Cognitive Approaches to Literature and Culture).* Austin: University of Texas Press 2010.

– *Of Literature and Knowledge: Explorations in Narrative Thought Experi-*

ments, Evolution, and Game Theory. New York and London: Routledge 2007.

– *A Stanislaw Lem Reader (Rethinking Theory).* Evanston, IL: Northwestern University Press 1997.

Teuscher, Christof, ed. *Alan Turing: Life and Legacy of a Great Thinker.* Berlin: Springer 2004.

Tomasello, Michael. "The Human Adaptation for Culture." *Annual Review of Anthropology* 28 (1999): 509–29.

– *Origins of Human Communication.* Boston: MIT Press 2010.

– *Why We Cooperate.* Boston: MIT Press 2009.

Tomasello, Michael, Malinda Carpenter, Josep Call, Tanya Behne, and Henrike Moll. "Understanding and Sharing Intentions: The Origins of Cultural Cognition." *Behavioral and Brain Sciences* 28 (2005): 675–735.

Traiger, Saul. "Making the Right Identification in the Turing Test." *Minds and Machines* 10, no. 4 (2000): 561–72.

Turing, Alan. "Computing Machinery and Intelligence." In *Minds and Machines,* edited by Alan Ross Anderson. Englewood Cliffs, NJ: Prentice-Hall 1964. First published 1950.

– "Intelligent Machinery, A Heretical Theory: Report, National Physical Laboratory." Reprinted in *Machine Intelligence* 5 (1970): 3–23.

– "On Computable Numbers, with an Application to the *Entscheidungsproblem.*" *Proceedings of the London Mathematical Society* 42, no. 2 (1936): 230–65.

Turkle, Sherri. *Life on the Screen: Identity in the Age of the Internet.* New York: Simon & Schuster 1995.

Vallverdú, Jordi, and David Casacuberta, eds. *Handbook of Research on Synthetic Emotions and Sociable Robotics: New Applications in Affective Computing and Artificial Intelligence.* New York: IGI Global 2009.

Young, Jeffrey R. "Programmed for Love." *Chronicle Review,* 14 January 2001. http://chronicle.com/article/Programmed-for-Love-The/125922/?sid=wb&utm_source=wb&utm_medium=en.

Wakefield, Jane. "When Algorithms Control the World." 23 August 2011. http://www.bbc.co.uk/news/technology-14306146.

Watz, Marius. "Computer-Generated Writing." January 1997. http://www.xbeat.net/ware/poezak/ComputerGeneratedWriting.htm.

Weizenbaum, Joseph. *Computer Power and Human Reason: From Judgment to Calculation.* San Francisco: W.H. Freeman 1976.

Whitby, Blay. "Why the Turing Test Is AI's Biggest Blind Alley." 1997. http://www.informatics.sussex.ac.uk/users/blayw/tt.html.

Wiener, Norbert. *God and Golem Inc.* Cambridge, MA: MIT Press 1964.

Wigner, Eugene. "The Unreasonable Effectiveness of Mathematics in the Natural Sciences." *Communications in Pure and Applied Mathematics* 13 (1960): 1–14.

Williams, J.H.G., A. Witen, T. Suddendorf, and D.I. Perrett. "Imitation, Mirror Neurons and Autism." *Neuroscience and Behavioral Review* 25 (2001): 287–95

Wilson, Timothy D., Christopher Houston, Kathryn Etling, and Nancy Brekke. "A New Look at Anchoring Effects: Basic Anchoring and Its Antecedents." *Journal of Experimental Psychology: General* 4 (1996): 387–402.

Wittgenstein, Ludwig. *Philosophical Investigations.* Oxford: Basil Blackwell 1953.

– *Tractatus Logico-Philosophicus.* Translated by Brian McGuiness and David Pears. New York: Routledge.

Yang, A.C.C., C.K. Peng, H.W. Yien, and A.L. Goldberger. "Information Categorization Approach to Literary Authorship Disputes." *Physica A* 329 (2003): 473–83.

Index